New Curriculum

Primary English
Learn, practise and revise

Les Ray and Gill Budgell

Year **5**

Contents

RISING STARS

Content grid

Links to English Programme of Study for Key Stage 2

	Unit title	Objective	Focus	Speak about it
1	Word origins	Knowledge of word origins (morphology and etymology)	Word reading, spelling and word structure	Derivation
2	Transforming words – prefixes	Verb prefixes	Word reading, spelling and word structure	Prefixes
3	Transforming words – suffixes	Converting nouns or adjectives into verbs using suffixes	Word reading, spelling and word structure	Suffixes
4	Grouping words according to meaning	Apply growing knowledge of root words, prefixes and suffixes	Word reading, spelling and word structure	Derivation
5	Making notes to explain things	Understand what is read by: a) building on the skills developed in Years 3 and 4, and b) discussing and summarising main ideas and identifying key supporting details	Comprehension, composition and text structure	Making notes
6	Test your grammar, punctuation and spelling	• Making verbs from nouns and adjectives • Use of commas • Commas to clarify meaning • Adding prefixes • Adding suffixes		
7	Narrative techniques	In writing narratives, consider how authors have developed characters and settings in what they have read, listened to or seen performed	Comprehension, composition and text structure	Setting and place
8	Creating atmosphere	In narratives, describe settings, characters and atmosphere to convey character and advance the action	Comprehension, composition and text structure	Creating an atmosphere
9	Audience and purpose: planning	Plan writing by identifying the audience for and purpose of the writing, selecting the appropriate form and using other similar texts as models for their own writing	Comprehension, composition and text structure	Comparing texts
10	Structure of narrative texts – story structure	Plan writing by identifying the audience for and purpose of the writing, selecting the appropriate form and using other similar texts as models for their own writing	Comprehension, composition and text structure	Story elements and cartoons
11	News reports	Plan writing by identifying the audience for and purpose of the writing, selecting the appropriate form and using other similar texts as models for their own writing	Comprehension, composition and text structure	Discuss purpose, audience and features; newspaper reports
12	Instructions	Plan writing by identifying the audience for and purpose of the writing, selecting the appropriate form and using other similar texts as models for their own writing	Comprehension, composition and text structure	Discuss purpose, audience and features; instructions
13	Test your grammar, punctuation and spelling	• Relative clauses using *who, which, where* and *why* • Hyphens • Dashes to add a comment or information • Spelling confusable words • Silent letters		
14	Relative clauses	Relative clauses beginning with *who, which, where, why, whose, that* or with an implied (i.e. omitted) relative pronoun	Sentence structure and composition	Clauses

	Unit title	Objective	Focus	Speak about it
15	Letters	Plan writing by identifying the audience for and purpose of the writing, selecting the appropriate form and using other similar texts as models for their own writing	Comprehension, composition and text structure	Letters
16	Performing for meaning	Prepare poems and plays to read aloud and to perform, showing understanding through intonation, tone and volume so that the meaning is clear to an audience	Comprehension, composition and text structure	Reading and responding to poetry
17	Edit and improve your work	Propose changes to grammar, vocabulary and punctuation to enhance effects and clarify meaning	Sentence structure and composition	Editing and improving writing
18	How authors use language	Discuss and evaluate how authors use language, including figurative language, considering the impact on the reader	Comprehension, composition and text structure	Terminology, usage, purpose and effect
19	Use of direct speech	In narratives, describe settings, characters and atmosphere and integrate dialogue to convey character and advance the action	Comprehension, composition and text structure	Terminology: speech
20	Test your grammar, punctuation and spelling	• Cohesion within paragraphs • Brackets to add a comment or information • Brackets to explain the meaning of a word • Plurals • Homophones		
21	Common errors	Homophones and other words that are often confused	Word reading, spelling and word structure	Terminology: homophones
22	Finding new words	Use a thesaurus	Comprehension, composition and text structure	Terminology: adverbs and adjectives
23	Paragraphs and order	Link ideas across paragraphs using adverbials of time (e.g. later), place (e.g. nearby) and number (e.g. secondly)	Comprehension, composition and text structure	Terminology, usage, purpose and effect
24	Changing the order of sentences	Evaluate and edit by assessing the effectiveness of their own and others' writing	Comprehension, composition and text structure	Terminology, usage, purpose and effect
25	Speech marks (inverted commas)	Revision: proposing changes to grammar, vocabulary and punctuation to enhance effects and clarify meaning	Comprehension, composition and punctuation	Terminology, usage, purpose and effect
26	Apostrophes	Revision: proposing changes to grammar, vocabulary and punctuation to enhance effects and clarify meaning	Comprehension, composition and punctuation	Terminology, usage, purpose and effect
27	Dashes or brackets	Use dashes or brackets	Comprehension, composition and punctuation	Terminology: dashes and brackets Usage, purpose and effect
28	Test your grammar, punctuation and spelling	• Modal verbs • Adverbs • Punctuation of speech (revision) • Parenthesis • Useful words • Easily confused words		

1 Word origins

The derivation of place names

When people conquered areas of the British Isles they brought their language and culture with them. This happened with Celtic, Roman (bringing Latin and Greek), Anglo-Saxon, Norse and French invaders and settlers.

Adapted from *The Cambridge Encyclopedia of Language*

The original word	Language	Meaning	What we recognise of the word today
Beorg	Anglo-Saxon	hill, burial-mound	borough, burgh
Brycg	Anglo-Saxon	bridge	brig, bridge
Burh	Anglo-Saxon	fortified place	bur, borough, burgh, bury
Burna	Anglo-Saxon	stream, spring	bourne, burn, borne
Bær	Old Norse	farm, township	by
Caer	Welsh	fortified place	car
Ceaster	Latin	roman town, fort	chester, castor, caistor
Dalr	Old Norse	dale, valley	dal, dale
Dun	Anglo-Saxon	hill, down	dun, down, don, ton
Ham	Anglo-Saxon	homestead, village	ham
Ing	Anglo-Saxon	place of, group of people	ing
Stede	Anglo-Saxon	place, site	sted, stead
Strata	Latin	Roman road	strat, stret, streat, street
Tun	Anglo-Saxon	enclosure, village	ton, town

David Crystal

Birm + **ing** + **ham** – village of the people of Birm

Strat + **ton** – village on a Roman road

Car + **diff** – fort on the River Taff

Stan + **sted** – site of the stone

Speak about it

What does **derivation** mean?
How does knowing the origin of words help you to know what place names mean?
Which words in English do you know that come from another language?
Where can you find out about the derivation of words?

Comprehension

1) List the two Anglo-Saxon words meaning **hill**.

2) Which words came originally from Old Norse?

3) Which words come from Latin?

4) How many words originally come from Welsh?

5) Explain how you can work out the derivation of the name of Birmingham?

6) What other place names can you think of that use the source word meaning **farm** or **township**?

7) Look in an atlas to find more place names using these source words.

 Language focus

1) Using the information in this unit, write about the derivation of these place names.

   a. Caistor-by-the-sea   **b.** Ross-on-Wye   **c.** Middlesborough   **d.** Doncaster

   An atlas will help. Say something about which language the words come from and how you were able to work out the meaning.

2) Many names of places in the world come from other languages and histories. What can you find out about the derivation of these places?

   a. Los Angeles   **b.** San José   **c.** New York   **d.** Queensland   **e.** Waterloo

3) Explain how knowing something about derivation helps us to understand the meaning of words – and even how to spell them.

 Links to writing

1) Plan and carry out a class survey about where people live in your area. What can you work out about the derivation of the local place names?

2) Write a mystery story that involves the understanding of the meaning of place names on a map. How does the treasure get found in the end? Who has the evidence to work out the clues? You could include some local place names or use the information in this unit to invent some places.

2 Transforming words – prefixes

Prefixes go at the beginning of a word to change its meaning.

Prefixes can tell you what words mean.

re- means **back** or **again**,
e.g. **return**, **regain**, **reuse**

over- suggests **across**, **higher than**
or **too much** of something,
e.g. **overcome**, **overheat**, **overweight**

You can make a word mean its opposite (make it negative).

appear – **dis**appear

behave – **mis**behave

forest – **de**forest

Speak about it

What is a **prefix**?
How is it different from a suffix?
If you make a word mean its opposite, what happens to the spelling of the word?
Can you think of any other examples?
Many prefixes come from languages other than English. What countries would these be?
Do you know any tricks for learning to spell words where prefixes have been added?

Comprehension

1) Identify the prefixes in these words.

   a. regain   **b.** overheat   **c.** disappear   **d.** deforest   **e.** misbehave

2) Now identify the root words of the words above.

3) Are these root words whole or just parts of words? How does this help you spell the words?

Language focus

1) Give the opposites of these words, adding the prefixes **dis-**, **mis-**, or **de-** where possible.

manage	camp	appear	compose
classify	fortune	apply	appoint
approve	advantage	conduct	fuse

2) Which of the following words are not correct? Give the correct spelling. Explain what the rule should be.

dissagree	misscalculate
recapture	overdevelop
definite	remove

3) Write these words using the correct prefixes **over-** or **re-**. Which words can use both? How does the prefix change the meaning?

balance	estimate
ground	activate
make	classify
check	animate
charge	connect
board	

Links to writing

1) Write a paragraph. Then use prefixes to make it mean the opposite. Choose your words carefully, e.g. **He agreed (disagreed) with his mum because she liked (disliked) his guitar playing.**

2) Make a set of rules to display in your classroom giving spelling hints to use when you are transforming words with prefixes.

3 Transforming words – suffixes

Suffixes go at the end of words to change their meaning.

Look at these three suffixes.

-ate

-ise

-ify

You can change nouns and adjectives into verbs using suffixes.

The suffix is used to form verbs with the meaning 'cause to be'.

Noun	Verb
magnet	to magnetise
identity	to identify
investigation	to investigate
advert	to advertise
acceleration	to accelerate
note	to notify

Adjective	Verb
simple	to simplify
visual	to visualise
circular	to circulate
final	to finalise
valid	to validate
pure	to purify

Speak about it

What is a **suffix**?

If you add a suffix to the end of a word, does it change the spelling of the original root of the word?

Can you think of any examples?

How is a suffix different from a prefix?

Do you know any tricks for learning to spell words where suffixes have been added?

How can some suffixes change the meaning of a word?

Comprehension

1) Identify the suffixes in the words on the opposite page.

2) Identify the root form of these words.

3) When you add a suffix to the root form of the word to change the word form (e.g. verb to noun), does the spelling of the word change? How?

4) Break the words opposite down into their syllables, e.g. **mag – net – ise**.

5) Do you know any rules that would help when adding suffixes? What happens, for instance, if you have to add a suffix to a word ending in -e?

Language focus

1) Write the following words adding the suffix **-ify**. Check your spelling in a dictionary. What changes to the words do you have to make?

| class | note | identity | simple | mystery | unite |

2) Make verbs of the following by adding the correct suffix. What changes to the words do you have to make? Do you notice anything that might help you write a rule?

| magnet | complication | symbol | education | vision |
| special | demonstration | calculation | refrigerator | character |

3) Find one meaning for each of the following words. Write them in sentences to show that you understand them.

| verify | pollinate | duplicate |
| estimate | fortify | qualify |

Links to writing

1) There are other ways of transforming words. Form nouns from the following adjectives.

   a. loyal   **b.** good   **c.** high

   What changes do you notice in the spelling of the words?

2) Form verbs from the following nouns.

   a. knee   **b.** spark   **c.** clean

   What changes do you notice in the spelling of the words?

3) Make a poster to display in your classroom that gives spelling hints when you are using suffixes to transform words. Use a computer to do this.

4 Grouping words according to meaning

You can group some words because they contain the same prefix.

The prefix will probably come from Latin or Greek. It should help you with the meaning of the word.

auto	autograph autobiography	(**auto-** means **self**)
circ	circulate circumference	(**circ-** means **around**)
bi	bisect bicycle	(**bi-** means **two**)
tele	telephone television	(**tele-** means **from afar**)

Some words contain a root of an ancient word.

This will help you to group them.

graph photograph	(*graphein* is an ancient Greek word meaning **to write**)
microscope microlight	(**micro-** comes from an ancient Greek word meaning **small**)
decimal decade	(**dec-** comes from the Greek word *deka* meaning **ten**)

Speak about it

Many English words come from other languages. Which languages do you think have had the biggest effect on English?

How can knowing the derivation of words help you to spell them?

Where might you find out more about the derivation of words and how this can help you with spelling?

Which parts of words make it easier for you to group words: beginnings (prefixes), middles (roots) or ends (suffixes)?

Comprehension

1) Some words in this unit are very difficult. Write down the meanings of all the words, using a dictionary when necessary.

2) Why is it helpful to know something of the derivation of words if you want to group them?

3) Break the words opposite down into syllables. This will make you concentrate on one part of the word at a time. Do you recognise any patterns in your groups?

4) Separate the prefixes from the roots of the words. Which words do you recognise? Can you guess what their prefixes mean, e.g. how many wheels does a bicycle have?

5) Does your dictionary say anything about where the words originally came from?

Language focus

1) Find some more words that you could add to groups of words containing the prefixes opposite, e.g. **auto- circ- bi- tele- trans-**

2) The prefix **con-** means **together**. Say what these words mean.
   a. congregation   **b.** connect   **c.** constellation

3) Make as many words as you can with each of the following prefixes. Their meaning is in brackets.
   a. uni- (one)   **b. tri-** (three)   **c. quad-** (four)

4) Find one word beginning with **ex-** for each of the following.
   a. to cry out   **c.** to trade goods with another country
   b. to breathe out   **d.** to put out a fire

Links to writing

1) **Micro** comes from a Greek word meaning **small**. Use a dictionary and find three words to group containing this root.

2) **Manu** comes from a Latin word meaning **hand**. Use a dictionary and find three words to group containing this root.

3) Use all these words in sentences to show that you know what they mean.

4) Give one word beginning with **sur-** for each of the following.
   a. the top of the water   **c.** a person who escapes from a shipwreck
   b. to give in during a fight   **d.** an amount of something that is left over

5 Making notes to explain things

People in ancient times supposed that the Earth was something like a flat disc, surrounded by a 'moat' of ocean, over which rotated the star-spangled dome of the heavens. Beyond the moat were huge mountains that supported the heavens. Beyond the dome was a heaven composed of water – some of which came down as rain, through trap doors. The sun, as a god in his chariot, crossed the sky every day. Below the Earth was Hades, the place for the dead – also surrounded by water.

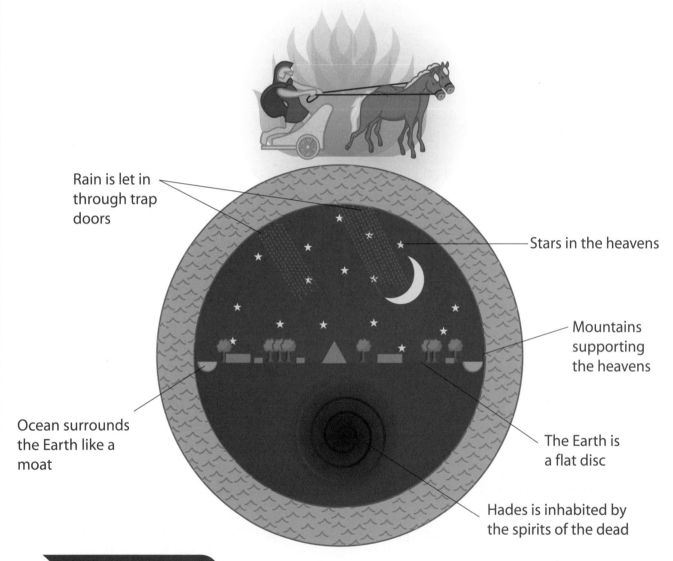

Rain is let in through trap doors

Stars in the heavens

Mountains supporting the heavens

Ocean surrounds the Earth like a moat

The Earth is a flat disc

Hades is inhabited by the spirits of the dead

Speak about it

Why do people make notes?
What notes do you make at home?
What notes do you make at school?
How can a diagram be more useful than a page of words?
Would the diagram be as useful if there were no labels?
In what way is this picture of the world different from the one you learn about in geography?

Comprehension

1) What shape did people in ancient times think the world was?

2) What did they think it was surrounded by?

3) How did they think the rain was caused?

4) Where did they think the sunlight came from?

5) How did they explain the heavens not falling down?

6) What did they believe was underneath the Earth?

Language focus

1) Find the text in the passage for which labels are given in the diagram. Is anything missed out? Which is easier to understand – the passage of text or the diagram? Why?

2) Here are some notes from a shopping list. Write them out in at least four sentences, as a paragraph, starting 'You will need …'. Decide which version – the notes or the paragraph – is best for its purpose. Why?

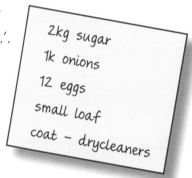

2kg sugar
1k onions
12 eggs
small loaf
coat – drycleaners

3) Make notes from the passage on the opposite page, using abbreviations, to produce a shorter version in a paragraph. Is this easier to understand than the diagram given?

Links to writing

1) Read through the passage opposite and pick out the most important (key) words. Write these down and use them as the centre of a spider diagram to which you can add notes. Underline key words in colour on your diagram.

2) It is important that you put notes into your own words. Write out the notes on the diagram in your own words, finding different words for **heavens**, **supporting**, **disc**, **inhabited**, **surrounds**, **ocean**.

3) Ask yourself questions about a passage from a geography or a history book you are using in class. Who? What? Where? When? Why? Write notes to answer your questions.

6 Test your grammar, punctuation and spelling

Grammar

Making verbs from nouns and adjectives

Rewrite each noun as a verb and use it in a sentence.

1) horror

2) creation

3) advert

4) significant

5) apology

6) organisation

7) electricity

8) revision

Punctuation

Use of commas

Rewrite these sentences, using commas in the correct places.

1) Pancakes by the way are made from flour milk eggs and flavouring.

2) The poster said that 'The Big Bears' they're rubbish in any case were all a sell-out.

3) Jack's brother he's the one who is brilliant at football invited me to join the team.

4) On my shopping list I have chocolates always those orange ones ice cream bread and posh crisps.

5) Abi ate a burger large of course a medium drink a medium bag of fries and an apple turnover before she went for a run and felt sick.

6) In the box there were piles of photographs ancient dirty unloved and dog-eared and worth nothing.

Commas to clarify meaning

Add commas to the sentences (or just to one if a comma is not needed for both) to give different meanings to each.

1) Whilst reading a poster I noticed the bus had arrived.
   Whilst reading a poster I noticed the bus had arrived.

2) Attention to the toilets.
   Attention to the toilets.

3) After we left Dad Mum my sister and I could not stop laughing.
   After we left Dad Mum my sister and I could not stop laughing.

4) Sal teased the little dog with the big bone.
   Sal teased the little dog with the big bone.

5) Tom walked on his hands working faster than normal.
   Tom walked on his hands working faster than normal.

6) No eating please.
   No eating please.

Spelling

Adding prefixes

Add a prefix to change the word. These may help you: **en-**, **mis-**, **under-**, **bi-**, **im-**, **un-**, **de-**.

Example   suitable → unsuitable

1) possible
2) understand
3) ground

4) circle
5) annual
6) activate

Adding suffixes

Add a suffix to change the word. These may help you: **-ion**, **-tion**, **-ssion**, **-ist**, **-able**, **-al**.

Example   progress → progression

1) permit
2) tour
3) reflect

4) believe
5) create
6) symmetry

7 Narrative techniques

From *The Peppermint Pig*

'Walk up, walk up, ladies and gentlemen, chance of a lifetime to see the World's Fattest Lady. Satisfaction guaranteed, only sixpence.' The booths had raised platforms in front with pictures of what was on show inside and men shouting their wares. 'Roll up, roll up, see the Marvel of Nature, the Elephant Man with a Genuine Trunk.' The men were called barkers, Aunt Harriet said, and you

couldn't believe all they said: she had seen the Elephant Man the year before last and there was nothing marvellous about him at all, he only had an extra long nose.

Naphtha flames roared and shivered and flared yellow ribbons of flame on the wind, lighting up gingerbread stalls where gingerbread houses they sold spread with white icing; hoop-la and coconut shies; the booth where you could have a tooth pulled for sixpence or watch it being done to someone else for a penny; and best and most beautiful, the big merry-go-round with its sailing horses and peacocks and unicorns, and its sweet grinding tune that played on and on …

They went on the merry-go-round. Theo on a prancing horse with flaring red nostrils and Poll on an ostrich. The seat was slippery and she clutched at its neck while she swooped and soared and the music played *Polly Redwing* and the coloured world flew faster and faster. She saw her mother and shouted, 'Look at me, look at me,' and drummed her feet on the side of the ostrich, but the next time round mother had vanished. Theo cried out, 'Look, Poll, look …' craning round so he almost fell off his horse. He was red-faced and crowing with laughter. 'Look, *Jonnie*,' he screamed, and as the merry-go-round began to slow down, Poll saw their pig galloping past, Mother and George running after him.

Nina Bawden

Speak about it

Do all stories have a **setting**?

Does a setting have to be a **place**?

What senses do we have to appeal to if we want to give a sense of place?

Comprehension

1) Why do you think the booths had raised platforms in the front?

2) What were the men called who shouted out the attractions?

3) What proof can you give to show that these men did not always tell the truth?

4) What did the author think was the best and most beautiful attraction? Why?

5) Give two reasons why Poll found it difficult to hang on.

6) What did Theo see that made him laugh so much?

Language focus

1) What would you expect a fairground to be like? Make a list of important features you would need to create the setting for your reader.

2) List details from the passage that concentrate on noise and colour. How do these make the place more interesting for the reader?

3) Complete a chart to show how these details appeal to the senses of the reader, so they can imagine the setting more easily.

Sound	
Taste	
Sight	
Touch	

4) Identify examples of alliteration, metaphors and personification that have been used to create the atmosphere. Look at the comparisons used.

Links to writing

1) Continue with the story of Poll and Theo at the fair, using details to make the setting real for the reader.

   What other things will there be at the fair?

   Where else do they go at the fair?

2) Imagine they return to the fair during the day when it is raining. Describe the scene.

   How is it different?

   How do you make the setting interesting for the reader?

   Use appropriate detail to appeal to your reader's five senses.

8 Creating atmosphere

From *The Amazing Mr Blunden*

The wet daffodils shone in a golden heap in the grey trug as Lucy came up the path from the lake. The gravel that crunched beneath her feet was full of sprouting weeds and moss grew in the shady patches. The whole garden was badly neglected but it still had a wild beauty. Now that the summer is coming, thought Lucy, I'll get Jamie to help me tidy it up a bit.

She took a short cut through the overgrown ruins at the east end of the house and stopped to look up at the pointed window arches that stood out like bones against the sky. Like the bones of a bird in the gutter, she thought; all that is left of a long-dead building. She could see that it had once been the wing of a house, but the soaring arches seemed to be of some older style, perhaps some abbey, destroyed by Henry the Eighth. Clumps of herbs had spread from the garden into the ruins: thyme and marjoram which gave off a sweet, wet scent underfoot. There were wallflowers too, high up on the stonework, and she added to her basket the few that were in her reach.

Beyond the ruins, a gravel path wound its way into the shrubbery and she went in search of the rhododendron …

Lucy began to feel strangely drowsy as though the scent of the rhododendron were a sweet, heavy drug. Her mind seemed to be growing still and empty almost as if it had stuck in a groove from which she was unable to move it …

Then she sensed that there was something moving through the mist on the lawn, just beyond the point at which her eyes were focused. She could not see very clearly, but it seemed to be two pale figures and they were moving towards her slowly and with purpose.

Fear gripped her.

Antonia Barber

> **trug** – basket for collecting flowers

Speak about it

What do you understand by **an atmosphere** in a piece of writing?
Under what kind of circumstances would you create an atmosphere in your writing?
Why is it important to appeal to your reader's senses when you are trying to create an atmosphere?
What senses would you appeal to? Why?

Comprehension

1) What flowers has Lucy been collecting? What does this tell us about the time of year?

2) What sort of windows did the ruins have?

3) What period did she think they were from?

4) What did they remind Lucy of?

5) How did Lucy know that herbs grew there?

6) How did Lucy begin to feel strange? What really scared her?

Language focus

1) What kind of atmosphere has the author created? Investigate how the structure of the passage helps.

2) Find details to illustrate these. Say what kind of atmosphere is created in each part.

   a. beautiful silent scene   **b.** walking through ruined building   **c.** feels drowsy

3) Copy and complete the chart. Use detail from the passage to show how the author appeals to your senses.

Detail	Touch	Taste	Sight	Hearing	Smell
Wet daffodils	Yes		Yes		

4) Identify any similes that create the atmosphere when Lucy is walking through the ruined building. How does the final sentence add tension?

5) Explain how you have to understand what the character is feeling to get the most from the atmosphere.

Links to writing

1) Write your own story, creating atmosphere. Use the same structure as this passage to help. Set your story at night. Think about: what kind of atmosphere do you want to create? What era will your story be set in? When and where will the story be set? Which senses will your detail appeal to? Use a chart like the one above to collect details before you write.

2) Now write the same story, but include dialogue. What kind of things will people need to say to create the atmosphere? What new detail do you need to create the atmosphere?

9 Audience and purpose: planning

Here are two passages about tropical storms and
their effects. How did the authors plan their material?
Let's investigate the differences between them.

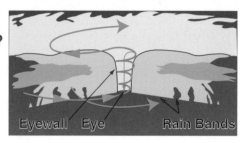

Eyewall   Eye   Rain Bands

A

Tropical cyclones – what are they?

- Produce extremely strong and powerful winds
- Tornadoes, torrential rain, high waves, storm surge
- Created over large bodies of warm water

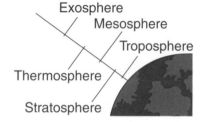

Exosphere
Mesosphere
Troposphere
Thermosphere
Stratosphere

Effects

- Lose their strength over land – why coastal regions
  can receive huge damage – inland regions safe from
  receiving strong winds
- Heavy rains can produce flooding inland
- Storm surges can produce extensive coastal flooding up to 40 km inland

Good or bad?

- Bad effects on humans and property but can also relieve drought conditions
- They carry heat away from the tropics – important mechanism of the global
  atmospheric circulation – help maintain balance in the Earth's troposphere

B

From *High Wind in Jamaica*

The wind by now was more than redoubled. The shutters were bulging as if tired
elephants were leaning against them, and Father was trying to tie the fastening with
his handkerchief. But to push against the wind was like pushing against rock. The
handkerchief, shutters, everything burst: the rain poured in like the sea into a sinking
ship, the wind occupied the room, snatching pictures from the wall, sweeping the table
bare. Through the gaping frames the lightning-lit scene without was visible. The creepers,
which before had looked like cobwebs, now streamed up into the sky like new-combed
hair. Bushes were lying flat, laid back on the ground as close as a rabbit lays his ears.
Branches were leaping about loose in the sky.

Richard Hughes

Speak about it

What are the main differences between these two passages?
Who would their audiences be? What are they trying to do?
Where do you think the authors got their information from?

Comprehension

1) From text A, list what tropical cyclones can bring with them.

2) Explain why coastal regions sometimes get all the damage from cyclones, but inland areas remain safe.

3) Name one good thing brought about by tropical cyclones mentioned in text A.

4) In text B, how are the shutters described?

5) When the wind got in the room, what kind of things did it do?

6) What did it do to the vegetation outside?

Language focus

1) What is the author's aim in text A? What kinds of features does the author use to make planning easier and make clear the ideas in his notes?

2) Investigate how the author of text A develops ideas. You may find that completing a chart will help.

Idea	Developments
Tropical cyclones – what are they?	

3) In text B, what kind of plan do you think the author has used? List the points in order, e.g. **1. The wind**, **2. The shutters**.

Links to writing

1) Research about tropical rainforests and make notes. Use sub-headings, bullet points and numbered points to make your ideas clear.

2) Use the same notes to write a paragraph or two from a story about being lost in the forest. You will have to plan this in a different way.

What happens?

Who is involved?

How do characters feel?

How do you refine your ideas by using description?

10 Structure of narrative texts – story structure

Dennis the Menace

© D.C. Thomson & Co. Ltd.

Speak about it

Stories should at least have a beginning, middle and end. Try to work with a beginning, a build up, a problem, a resolution and an end. Which part do you think this extract comes from?

What clues are there to tell you this?

What would happen if a story did not have a build up?

Would you be happy if a story did not have a resolution?

Cartoons use very few words to tell a story. How else do they give you a sense of what is going on?

Think about the 'theme' of Dennis the Menace. How many other characters can you think of that are like this sort of character and have this sort of theme?

Comprehension

1) Who are the main characters in this story?

2) Give some evidence to show that the story starts with some action.

3) What device in this cartoon makes the story develop?

4) What is going to happen next?

5) How do you think it will end?

Language focus

1) Continue the story in note form to make sure that you have a beginning, an extended middle and an end.

2) Cartoons are similar to **storyboards**. Plan out the story of a well-known fairy tale using only six pictures. Decide on the most important events and characters and what the order of the story should be.

3) Stories need conflict or problems – something needs to happen to make the character do something. Choose three well-known children's stories and write about the conflict in them. What does the main character do to overcome the problem? Does the main character always win in the end?

Links to writing

1) Here is a story with a structure.

   Once upon a time, there was a thirsty man on a sofa. He got up off the sofa, went to his kitchen, searched through his refrigerator, found a bottle of water, drank it, and returned to his seat, thirst quenched.

   What is wrong with this story?

2) Improve on the story. Start by asking yourself some questions about your main character, what might happen to him and how he will react.

   Who is your main character?
   What does your character look like?
   What is your character's personality?
   What will happen to your character and how will he react?

3) Now start adding other information. If you are using a computer, you can use the following list as a guide and edit, add and move text around on screen.

   action   background   conflict   development   end

11 News reports

Headline – the main idea of the report

Opening – Who? What? Where?

Body of text – the details

Sub-headings – key events

Other opinions – include quotations

Style – past tense; detail about who, what, when, where, how. Brief, catchy detail

Fred's ruler destroyed as it topples from table

Today, at a small city primary school, there was confusion and shock when a ruler toppled from a table and smashed on the floor.

The ruler, a new plastic one especially purchased for school to use in literacy class, belonged to short-haired Fred Savage – a Year 5 student at Admiral House Primary School in Docklands, and is now totally useless.

Knocked flying

When interviewed Fred stated, 'I'm in shock. It happened this morning. I was just starting to think about writing my story so I looked for my new ruler. It had disappeared.' He paused for a moment to recover his thoughts. The shocked and shaken Fred continued. 'Then I saw it on the table. I was relieved because I thought my friends were playing a joke. Suddenly, as I stood up, the books fell sideways and knocked it flying. I could do nothing about it.'

Year 4 boys to be interviewed

Fred's best mate, Andy – a lively dark-haired sporty type, also in Year 5 – told us in confidence that he thought the opposing football team in Year 4 must have deliberately positioned the books so this would happen. 'Fred is our best scorer and they knew he would be upset for the game tomorrow. How low can you sink?' he sneered accusingly.

Fred's teacher, Ms Smith (32, with long blonde hair), said that she was looking into the complaints by members of her class and would be interviewing certain Year 4 boys. The class was still in a state of shock, but the school has issued a request to the general public for anyone who knows more about this distressing matter to contact them as soon as possible.

Speak about it

What is the purpose of a newspaper report?

Who is the reader?

Why are headlines and sub-headings important?

Look for verbs describing actions. Why do they have to be so accurate?

Would a photograph help? Why?

Do you know if everything you read in a newspaper report is true?

Comprehension

1) Where did this event occur?

2) When did this event occur?

3) Whose ruler was it?

4) What detail shows you that Fred was shocked?

5) Who was a witness to the event?

6) What is Andy's opinion of what happened?

7) How did the teacher react?

Language focus

1) Write some more headlines for this story giving different views – was it the fault of Year 4, or someone else?

2) Find examples of headlines in other newspapers and say if you think they summarise the news story well.

3) Look at the style features of a newspaper report on the opposite page. Pick out examples of each.

4) Is the report written in the correct time order? Find evidence of the cohesive devices used to help the paragraphs to flow.

5) Pick out the sub-headings. How do these help the paragraphs to flow? Would it be more difficult to read if they were not used?

Links to writing

1) Think of an important sports fixture. Write a report for the school newspaper as if you were there. Consider the following details.

   How will you introduce the scene? Who? What? Where? When? How? Why?

   What information will you include?

   Avoid using 'I' or 'me'.

   Whom will you interview and quote?

2) Use a computer to produce the newspaper article so that it looks like the real thing.

12 Instructions

CHOCOLATE BISCUITS

Get organised to make these wonderfully tasty chocolate biscuits in no time at all.

What you need

Materials or requirements to complete the task

- ¹/₂ cup of self-raising flour
- 1¹/₂ teaspoons of baking powder
- pinch of salt
- ¹/₂ cup of butter or margarine
- ¹/₂ cup of sugar
- 2 cups of grated chocolate
- 1 egg
- ¹/₂ cup of milk
- some cups for measuring
- 2 mixing bowls
- a fork
- a greased baking tray

What you do

What is the aim of the instructions?

1 First, mix together the flour, baking powder and salt in a mixing bowl.

2 Add the butter and use a fork to mix the ingredients together.

3 Stir in the sugar and grated chocolate.

Style – command verbs; use you; use connectives to do with time – then, first, now; be brief

4 In another bowl, beat an egg thoroughly with a fork.

5 Add the milk to the egg and mix them together.

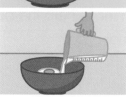

6 Pour the mixture of egg and milk into the flour mixture.

7 Now with your hands, knead the mixture lightly into a dough. If the mixture is very dry, add some more milk.

8 Divide the kneaded dough into small rounds.

9 Place the rounds on the greased baking tray.

10 Bake the biscuits in a hot oven until done (approximately 20 minutes).

Evaluation – has it worked?

After you have removed them from the tray, allow them to cool before eating. What do you think of them?

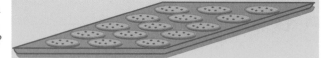

Speak about it

What is the purpose of instructions?

Why is stating the aim of the instructions important?

If there were no materials or requirements stated, would the instructions work? Why?

Can any instructions be written in any order? Think of some examples.

What kind of verbs are used in instructions?

How do you know if instructions are good or not?

Comprehension

1) Why is a title useful in a set of instructions?

2) Why are sub-headings useful? Write the sentences you would have to include if the sub-headings were not there. What difference does it make?

3) What other features on the opposite page make the instructions easy to use?

4) What would happen if the steps were not in sequence?

Language focus

1) Look at the style features of the instructions on the opposite page. Pick out examples of each from the recipe.

2) Commands are used in instructions. Make a list of all the one-word commands that you would use if you were training a dog.

3) Instructions use connectives to help you to follow a logical process. These include **then**, **first**, **now**. Rewrite some of the instructions removing the numbers and using these words. What difference does it make? Is it easier to read and to follow or more difficult?

Links to writing

1) Imagine that you have a new penfriend, from another country, who is interested in what you do at school. Write instructions (in simple English) to help him/her play a game or make something at school. Use these style tips.

Be brief and clear, but give all the right details.
Follow the right order.
Use link words (then, now) or numbers.
Use the present tense and command verbs.
Use technical vocabulary correctly.
Use 'accurate' description – give adjectives and adverbs in order to help the reader understand what to do.

2) Write instructions for a two-player game, e.g. 'Stone, Paper, Scissors'. Usually commands are written using the **you** form of the verb. Use examples of the third person, e.g. 'Player 1' and 'Player 2'.

3) Write a set of simple numbered instructions to help a young child tie shoelaces. You could draw diagrams to help.

13 Test your grammar, punctuation and spelling

Grammar

Relative clauses using *who*, *which*, *where* and *why*

Complete these sentences using the correct word.

1) The bird flew to her nest, _____ she settled cosily on her eggs.

2) The old woman, _____ told us the story, was very sad.

3) The plane, _____ flew faster than sound, was a new model.

4) In the *Harry Potter* books, Lord Voldemort is a character _____ is Harry's arch enemy.

5) The smoke, _____ was disgusting, came from the cigarette.

6) We met in the place _____ we had met before.

7) Leonardo da Vinci was the famous artist _____ painted the *Mona Lisa*.

8) He wouldn't talk about his life, _____ was the reason _____ we wanted to meet him.

Punctuation

Hyphens

Write a sentence for each of these hyphenated words.

1) short-tailed

2) ready-to-go

3) all-inclusive

4) sugar-free

5) power-mad

6) quick-tempered

Dashes to add a comment or information

Add dashes to the sentences to show where there is a comment or extra information.

1) This camera top of the range don't you know is on my birthday list.

2) We're off school this Friday we always have an inset day at this time of year so I can catch up then.

3) I love football I try really hard so I always get selected for the team.

4) Netball a game played more by girls than boys for some reason is so much fun.

5) Ellen the tall girl at the back with blonde hair is very popular in our class.

6) Lacrosse is a game they play at the school on the hill they would, wouldn't they but we play hockey.

Spelling

Spelling confusable words

Choose and write out the correct spelling for each one.

Example

nuisance   nuisence   nusance

1) availible   available   avalable

2) relevant   relavant   relevent

3) symbil   symbal   symbol

4) especially   especialy   esspecially

5) vegatible   vegetable   vegtible

6) vehicle   vehacle   vehecle

Silent letters

Spell the word for the pictures.

1)

2)

14 Relative clauses

Simple sentences can be boring in your writing. Often these are just one clause in length.

On the whole, sentences need to be more than one clause in length and they should be linked to make them interesting. You can do this by using relative pronouns – words such as:

who   which   where   why   whose   that

Here are two simple sentences.

He had a row with his mother. She was very cross.

This is one clause

This is another clause

It would be more interesting to say:

He had a row with his mother *who* was very cross.

You choose **who** because the subject of the sentence (mother) is a person.

This next sentence needs a different joining word (relative pronoun).

The teacher picked up the book. It had the cover torn off.

This is one clause

This is another clause

It would be better as:

The teacher picked up the book *which* had the cover torn off.

You choose **which** because the subject of the verb is an object (the book).

This next sentence has a person as the subject but you would use whose to join them because you mention something belongs to him in the second sentence (*his* caravan).

I knew a man. His caravan caught fire.

I knew a man *whose* caravan caught fire.

Speak about it

What is a clause?
How are they different from phrases?
Why is it not good just to use simple sentences in your writing?
Explain how the relative pronouns **who, which, where, why, whose** join one clause with another in a sensible way.
All these words are question words. How could this help you to add other interesting detail to your sentences?

Comprehension

1) Why do you think the sentences you make in this unit are called **complex sentences**?

2) What kind of information have you added by using these simple words? Think about whether this information has to do with time, places, people, things or events.

3) How does knowing this help you decide which of the relative pronouns to use?

4) Explain why the following sentences would be incorrect:

The teacher picked up the book **what** had the cover torn off.

He had a row with his mother **that** was very cross.

I made up my mind **what** I would like to go on my holiday.

Language focus

1) Use **who**, **which**, **where**, **why, whose** or **that** to join the following sentences. Explain why you made your choice.

   a. Reuben has a new girlfriend. She is a champion swimmer.

   b. I am going to see my sister. She is older than me.

   c. The tree blew in the wind. It had been blowing hard all day.

   d. He returned the t-shirt to the shop. It was too big for him.

   e. I talked to the girl. Her hair was bright red.

   f. He was sent to see the head teacher. She told him off.

   g. In the playground I saw John. His leg was in plaster.

   h. He could not understand. It had not happened to him.

   i. My uncle owns a car. It is always breaking down.

   j. The detectives never knew. The men had robbed the bank.

Links to writing

1) Use these relative pronouns in a more interesting way, e.g. **The girl was best at maths. She did badly in her exam.** Can be written as **The girl *who* was best at maths did badly in her exam.**

   a. The boy's arm was caught in the door. He struggled to get it free.

   b. The girl's bike had been lost. She phoned the police.

   c. The boxer was knocked out in the ring. He had not been good enough.

   d. The doctor had been on call. He arrived too late to deliver the baby.

   e. The computer game was broken. It had only been bought last week.

2) Many people use commas instead of relative pronouns and this is incorrect. Write out the following passage using the appropriate words.

   There was a man, he had black hair, he came towards me, it scared me.

15 Letters

Admiral House Primary School has been told that its local playing field is to be sold. New houses will be built on it.

> Admiral House Primary School
> Docklands
> Liverpool L7 3GS
> 19 January
>
> The Managing Director
> Customer Builders
> Stonard Road
> Manchester M22 8NB
>
> Dear Sir
> I am writing to tell you that my whole class (5B) is upset by the fact that you want to build houses on our playing field.
> We all enjoy PE and games, and this playing field is the only place the school has to carry out these activities. Where are we going to go when the houses have been built?
> Our teacher says that it is the law to teach PE but we will have nowhere to do this. We will have to hire a coach to get to a playing field miles away. This will be very expensive for our school and we are not very well off.
> What is more, we will also have to share this field with two other schools so we will not have so much time. Think of all the hours travelling in London traffic. This will mean we can spend less time doing important things like literacy.
> My mum says she will not be able to pick me up from this field after school because it is too far away from where she works. Other children in my class have the same problems.
> I hope you can understand our point of view and will reconsider your plans.
>
> Yours faithfully
> Dominic
>
> !!SAVE OUR SCHOOL PLAYING FIELD!!

Annotations:
- Your address here with the date
- The address of the person to whom you are sending this
- Each paragraph contains one argument
- Persuasive language: **what is more**; using questions
- Formal greeting and ending

Speak about it

What is the purpose of this letter?
How is it different from a letter you would send to a friend?
What features of style would you **not** use for this type of letter? Why?
If you are trying to persuade someone, what are the best ways of doing this in writing?
Has the writer persuaded you? Why?

English Study Guide: Year 5

Answer Booklet

1 Word origins
Comprehension
1) beorg, dun
2) by; dal, dale
3) chester, castor, caistor, strat, stret, streat, street
4) One – car
5) By breaking the word into syllables and finding the origins of those word parts.
6), 7) *Own answers*

Language focus
1) a. Caistor-by-the-sea means 'fort on the sea'.
   b. Ross-on-Wye means 'the town located on a headland on the river Wye'.
   c. Middlesborough means 'the fort between two towns'.
   d. Doncaster means 'a roman town, or a fort, on a hill'.
2) *Own answers*
3) If you know the original meaning and language the place name comes from, it might help you recognise spelling patterns.

Links to writing
1), 2) *Own answers*

2 Transforming words – prefixes
Comprehension
1) re; over; dis; de; mis
2) -gain, -heat, -appear, -forest, -behave
3) All whole words. Just add the prefix; do not change any other letters.

Language focus
1) mismanage, decamp, disappear, decompose, declassify, misfortune, disapply, misapply, disappoint, disapprove, disadvantage, misconduct, defuse
2) disagree, miscalculate. Just add the prefix to the original word. No need to change any spelling.
3) overbalance, rebalance, overestimate, re-estimate, overground, overactivate, reactivate, remake, reclassify, recheck, reanimate, recharge, overcharge, reconnect, overboard. The prefixes mean to do something again (re-) or to be more than (excess) (over-). Sometimes hyphens are used. Just add the prefix to the original word. No need to change any spelling.

Links to writing
1), 2) *Own answers*

3 Transforming words – suffixes
Comprehension
1) -ate, -ise, -ify
2) magnet-, identity-, investigation-, advert-, acceleration-, note-, simple-, visual-, circular-, final-, valid-, pure-
3) In most cases the spelling of the word doesn't change, but in some cases it does. The final, silent e is lost in words when adding a suffix beginning with a vowel. The final y becomes an i.
4) mag–net, mag–net–ise, i–den–ti–ty, i–den–ti–fy, in–ves–ti–ga–tion, in–ves–ti–gate, ad–vert, ad–ver–tise,

ac-cel-er-a-tion, ac-cel-er-ate, note, no-ti-fy sim–ple, sim–pli–fy, vi–su–al, vi–su–al–ise, cir–cu–lar, cir–cu–late
5) When you add *y* or a suffix that begins with a vowel to words ending in a silent e, you drop the e and add the suffix.
   When you add suffixes to words that end in *ge* or *ce*, do not drop the final e.
   The ending *ing* is a verb ending. When you add *ing* to words that end in *ie*, you drop the e and change the *y* to *i*. Then you add *ing*.
   When you add suffixes that do not end in vowels or *y*, you do not drop the final e.
   When you add suffixes that begin with a consonant, keep the final e if the suffix begins with a consonant.
   When you add the suffix *ment* to a word, the final e is dropped.
   There are always exceptions to rules!

Language focus
1) classify, notify, identify, simplify, mystify, unify
   Adding -ify to a final e would make a very different sound, so this is dropped and the word is sometimes changed.
2) to magnetise, to complicate, to symbolise, to educate, to visualise, to specialise, to demonstrate, to calculate, to refrigerate, to characterise
   -ion as the final suffix will usually be removed, and -ate added. Often two-syllable words ending in a consonant take -ise.
3)

verify – to confirm the truth	pollinate – placing pollen to fertilise a flower
duplicate – to make a copy	estimate – to judge the value or worth
fortify – to make stronger	qualify – to reach a level of competence

Links to writing
1) a. loyalty
   b. goodness
   c. highness
   There is no change in the spelling of these words but they add a suffix.
2) a. to kneel
   b. to spark
   c. to clean
   There is no change in the spelling of these words.
3) *Own answer*

4 Grouping words according to meaning
Comprehension
1) *Own answer*
2) The prefix or root might help you understand the meaning of the word.
3) aut–o–graph, aut–o–bi–og–ra–phy
   cir–cu–late, cir–cum–fer–ence
   bi–sect, bi–cy–cle
   tel–e–phone, tel–e–vis–ion
   graph, pho–to–graph
   mic–ro–scope, mic–ro–light
   dec–i–mal, dec–ade

Own answer
4) -graph, -biography, -late, -sect, -umference, -cycle, -phone, -vision, -graph, -scope, -light, -imal, -ade
   Auto means 'self', **circ** means 'circle', **bi** means 'two', **tele** means 'from afar', **graphein** means 'to write', **micros** means 'small', **dec** means 'ten'.
5) *Own answer*

Language focus
1) *Own answer*
2) a. **Congregation** means an assembly of persons brought together for common religious worship.
   b. **Connect** means to join, link or fasten together.
   c. **Constellation** means an easily recognised group of stars that appear to be located close together in the sky.
3) *Own answer*
4) a. exclaim
   b. exhale
   c. export
   d. extinguish

Links to writing
1), 2), 3) *Own answers*
4) a. surface
   b. surrender
   c. survivor
   d. surplus

5 Making notes to explain things
Comprehension
1) They thought the world was a flat disc.
2) They thought it was surrounded by a 'moat' of ocean.
3) They thought rain was water from heaven that came through trap doors.
4) They thought sunlight came from a god crossing the sky every day.
5) The heavens were supported by mountains.
6) They thought Hades was under the Earth.

Language focus
1) There is no label for the sun, as a god in his chariot, and there is no water surrounding Hades.
2), 3) *Own answers*

Links to writing
1), 2), 3) *Own answers*

6 Test your grammar, punctuation and spelling
Grammar
Making verbs from nouns or adjectives
1) horrify
2) create
3) advertise
4) signify
5) apologise
6) organise
7) electrify
8) revise

Punctuation
Use of commas
1) Pancakes, by the way, are made from flour, milk, eggs and flavouring.
2) The poster said that 'The Big Bears', they're rubbish in any case, were all a sell-out.
3) Jack's brother, he's the one who is brilliant at football, invited me to join the team.
4) On my shopping list I have chocolates, always those orange ones, ice cream, bread and posh crisps.
5) Abi ate a burger, large of course, a medium drink, a medium bag of fries and an apple turnover before she went for a run and felt sick.
6) In the box there were piles of photographs, ancient, dirty, unloved and dog-eared, and worth nothing.

Commas to clarify meaning
1) Whilst reading a poster, I noticed the bus had arrived.
   Whilst reading a poster I noticed the bus had arrived.
2) Attention, to the toilets.
   Attention to the toilets.
3) After we left, Dad, Mum, my sister and I could not stop laughing.
   After we left Dad, Mum, my sister and I could not stop laughing.
4) Sal teased the little dog, with the big bone.
   Sal teased the little dog with the big bone.
5) Tom walked on his hands, working faster than normal.
   Tom walked on, his hands working faster than normal.
6) No eating, please.
   No eating please.

Spelling
Adding prefixes
1) impossible
2) misunderstand
3) underground
4) encircle
5) biannual
6) deactivate

Adding suffixes
1) permission
2) tourist
3) reflection
4) believable
5) creation
6) symmetrical

7   Narrative techniques
Comprehension
1) The booths had platforms in front of them so that the pictures and 'barkers' could be seen better by the crowd.
2) 'barkers'
3) Aunt Harriet can prove that these men did not always tell the truth because she has seen the elephant man with a 'Genuine Trunk' and all he had was 'an extra long nose.'
4) The big merry-go-round was the 'best and most beautiful' attraction because of its fabulous creatures and beautiful music.
5) It was hard for Poll to cling on because the seat was slippery and the merry-go-round was moving quickly.
6) Theo saw his mother and George chasing after their pig.

Language focus
1) Own answer
2) 'men shouting', 'naphtha flames roared', 'yellow ribbons of flame', 'white icing', 'peacocks', 'sweet grinding tune', 'flaring red nostrils', 'music', 'coloured world', 'she saw her mother and shouted', 'Theo cried

out', 'He was red-faced and crowing', 'he screamed'. These descriptions make it much easier for the reader to imagine what the fair must have sounded like and looked like. They create a very noisy and bright atmosphere, just right for a description of a fairground.
3) **Sound**: barkers shouting, naphtha flames roaring, the sound of people having teeth removed perhaps, the music of the merry-go-round, the shouts of the children
   Taste: gingerbread with white icing, sweet grinding tune – this mixes the senses of sound and taste
   Sight: the booths with their platforms, the naphtha flames lighting up the gingerbread stalls, 'the coloured world'
   Touch: the slippery seat
4) Alliteration: 'swooped and soared'
   Metaphor: 'coloured world flew faster and faster'
   Personification: 'Naphtha flames roared and shivered'

Links to writing
1), 2) Own answers

8   Creating atmosphere
Comprehension
1) Lucy has been collecting daffodils so it must be spring.
2) The windows had arches that were 'pointed' and 'soaring'.
3) She thought they might be from the time of Henry the Eighth.
4) They reminded Lucy of 'the bones of a bird in the gutter'.
5) Lucy could smell the herbs.
6) The scent of the rhododendron made her start to feel drowsy. 'The two pale figures' moving towards her through the mist scared her.

Language focus
1) The atmosphere changes in the passage: It begins peacefully and calmly as Lucy collects her flowers; the ruins create an atmosphere of decay; the scent of the rhododendrons create a dreamlike, mysterious atmosphere; and finally, the figures in the mist create a tense, frightening atmosphere. The slow build up makes the arrival of the two pale figures more dramatic.
2), 3) Own answers
4) 'arches that stood out like bones' – the image of a skeleton.
   Drowsy – as if the scent were a drug. This seems to give an impression of unreality. Her mind – as if stuck in a groove, suggests she is not in control.
   The final sentence is short and sharp with no explanation.
5) The character is experiencing the events of the story through her five senses, so by understanding what the character is feeling we can get an idea of what the atmosphere must be like.

Links to writing
1), 2) Own answers

9   Audience and purpose: planning
Comprehension
1) Tropical cyclones can bring strong winds, tornadoes, heavy rain, waves and storms.
2) Inland areas stay safe because cyclones lose their strength over land.
3) Cyclones can relieve drought conditions or help to keep the Earth's atmosphere balanced by carrying heat away from the tropics.

4) The shutters are described as 'bulging as if tired elephants were leaning against them'.
5) The wind blew pictures from the walls and everything from the table.
6) Creepers 'streamed up into the sky', 'bushes were lying flat' and 'branches were leaping about loose'.

Language focus
1) The author is informing readers about tropical cyclones. A question is used to introduce the topic. There are other headings in bold and bullet points about different aspects of the topic, which give further information. There are diagrams to support the information. These features are not used in text B because the author's purpose is different. In text B the author is writing to describe.
2) In text A, each idea is presented as a heading in bold; the idea is then developed using bullet points.
3) 1. The wind
   2. The shutters
   3. Fixing the shutters
   4. The shutters break
   5. The wind in the room
   6. The scene outside
   7. The vegetation

Links to writing
1), 2) Own answers

10 Structure of narrative texts – story structure
Comprehension
1) Dennis the Menace and his dad.
2) The character shouts the instruction, 'Barricade the door!'
3) The story is divided into frames.
4) Dennis will attempt to solve the mystery.
5) Dennis will get into trouble but everything will end happily.

Language focus
1), 2), 3) Own answers

Links to writing
1) There is no conflict.
2), 3) Own answers

11 News reports
Comprehension
1) The event occurred at Admiral House Primary School in Docklands.
2) It occurred today.
3) The ruler belonged to Fred Savage.
4) 'there was confusion and shock'
   'When interviewed Fred stated, "I'm in shock."'
   'The shocked and shaken Fred continued.'
   'The class was still in a state of shock'
5) Apparently, there were no witnesses.
6) Andy suspects the Year 4 football team must have 'deliberately positioned the books so this would happen.'
7) She is looking into complaints by members of her class and will be interviewing certain Year 4 boys.

Language focus
1), 2), 3) Own answers
4) The event itself is in the correct time order, but interviews and comments look back on the event and reflect upon it.
   Devices include linking phrases, e.g. 'When interviewed ...', and the use of links back to Fred through the contacts interviewed.
5) There are two sub-headings: 'Knocked flying' and 'Year 4 boys to be interviewed'. They focus on the key events of the paragraph and aim to break up the text so

how much of the gold, silver or copper it contained.

6) Governments agree the value of a coin and that amount is stamped on it.

Language focus
1) The topic sentences are the first sentence in each paragraph: *own answers*
2) Each paragraph starts by mentioning a point in time, e.g.: *'Before'*, *'Even after'*, *'Eventually'*, *'The next stage'* and *'Today'*.
3) The text is written in a chronological narrative order. If you mix this order up, the passage no longer makes sense.
4) *Own answer*

Links to writing
1) *Own answer*

24 Changing the order of sentences
Comprehension
1) People were given surnames to help tell apart two people with the same first name. This information is in paragraph 3.
2) The word **surname** comes from the prefix sur- meaning 'over and above' or 'additional to'. This information is in paragraph 1.
3) Surnames were formed from either occupational names (paragraph 2) or from natural features (paragraph 3).
4) a. Johnson, because it is not an occupation.
   b. Brook, because it is not an occupation (Baxter means 'baker')
   c. Smith, because it is not a natural feature.

Language focus
1) Every other Monday I go to my Club, but we are moving soon to a new house.
   I think I will have to stop going because of the journey.
   It would be pleasant in summer but not good in winter, when the nights are cold and dark; especially if you like sitting in front of the TV like me.
2) The writer begins the paragraph with a question to introduce the main topic of the paragraph and make the reader think about the answer themselves. The other sentences in the paragraph go on to answer the question by giving further information and examples.
3) The order of sentences is important to guide the reader through the text logically.

Links to writing
1), 2), 3) *Own answers*

25 Speech marks (inverted commas)
Comprehension
1) The two characters speaking in the passage are Tom Sawyer and Huck Finn.
2) They met by the dead tree because they had come for their tools.
3) They don't go to the house because it is a Friday.
4) Their view of Friday is that it is an unlucky day.
5) This seems strange because it is very superstitious.
6) Huck had a dream about rats, which also concerned them.
7) The reader knows who is speaking each time because when there is a new speaker a new paragraph is started.

Language focus
1) New speaker, new paragraph
   Open and close speech marks
   Commas before speech starts
   Full stop or other final punctuation inside the speech marks

2) 'Look out!' warned the passenger.
   'What's the matter?' muttered the driver, half asleep.
   'Sorry,' the passenger answered apologetically, 'I thought you were going to crash.'
3) *Own answer*

Links to writing
1) *'There's some lucky days, maybe, but Friday ain't.'*
   Some days of the week are lucky, but Friday is not.
   By using Standard English rather than non-standard English, you lose the character's way of speaking and, therefore, their personality.
2), 3) *Own answer*

26 Apostrophes
Comprehension
1) The only two knights left are Sir Lucan and Sir Bedivere.
2) The two knights carried King Arthur to the deserted chapel in Camelot because he was dying.
3) King Arthur asks Sir Bedivere to take Excalibur and throw the sword into the lake.
4) When he tries to throw the sword away, a voice persuades him not to.
5) He tells King Arthur that the water rippled when he threw the sword into the lake, but nothing else.
6) King Arthur is furious and calls Sir Bedivere a liar and a traitor.

Language focus
Answers include:

1) Letters left out	Showing possession
He'd	Camelot's castles
We're	My time's short
Don't	His knight's vows

2) a. can't
   b. it's
   c. what's
   d. I've
   e. they've
   f. they're
3) a. the picture's frame
   b. a dog's collar
   c. the two ships' anchors
   d. the ladies' dresses
   e. the author's book
   f. many artists' paintings

Links to writing
1) a. The cat's kittens (one cat with lots of kittens)
      The cats' kittens (many cats with their kittens)
   b. My brother's books (the books belonging to one brother)
      My brothers' books (the books belonging to several brothers)
   c. The girl's dresses (the dresses belonging to one girl)
      The girls' dresses (the dresses belonging to several girls)
   d. The farmer's fields (the fields belonging to one farmer)
      The farmers' fields (the fields belonging to several farmers)
2) *Own answer*

27 Dashes and brackets
Comprehension
1) Mr Jingle's luggage consisted of a brown paper parcel.
2) Mr Jingle says that the rest of his luggage has already been sent ahead 'by water', meaning by boat.
3) He is trying to make himself seem more

important than he is by describing to the coachman the heavy and awkward luggage that has already been sent ahead. It is hard to believe him because all he seems to own is a shirt and a handkerchief.

4) He tells people to take care of their heads because the coach is about to pass under a low archway.
5) He tells how a tall woman had her head knocked off while eating sandwiches when she passed under the arch the other day.
6) The story is comic.
7) Mr Jingle likes to tell a good story and to shock people. He doesn't care about the truth of the story just so long as he can amaze his listeners.

Objective focus
1) 'Heads, heads, take care of your heads,' cried the stranger, as they came out under the low archway, which in those days formed the entrance to the coach-yard. 'This is a terrible and dangerous place. The other day, five children were travelling on this same coach with their mother. The mother was a tall lady, and as she sat here eating sandwiches she forgot about the low arch. The children heard a crash and a knock, looked around and saw their mother with her sandwich still in her hand, but no mouth to put it in. Her head had been completely taken off. Isn't that shocking?' **This** sounds less like spontaneous speech and more like a rehearsed recount. The story is less funny this way and we don't get a sense of Mr Jingle's distinctive, jerky way of speaking.
2) *Own answer*
3) I wanted to become a gospel singer (I had always sung gospel music with my father – he used to sing back home in Jamaica) so I joined a choir in south London.

Links to writing
1), 2), 3) *Own answers*

28 Test your grammar, punctuation and spelling
Grammar
Modal verbs
1) might
2) will
3) should
4) must
5) must
Adverbs
1) perhaps
2) arguably
3) probably
4) Surely
5) obviously

Punctuation
Punctuation of speech (revision)
1) 'Just mind where you are stacking those boxes,' said the woman.
2) 'Where would you like them stacked?' I asked.
3) 'Well, we usually have them taken upstairs,' she replied.
4) 'Not asking for much then,' I whispered under my breath.
5) 'Sorry, did you say something?' hissed the woman.

2) a. She gave me. (incorrect tense, using present instead of past) or She gives me.
b. the actors were (singular verb when it should be plural)
c. My mum doesn't let us (plural verb when it should be singular)
d. I never saw anyone (double negative)
e. Tracey did her work (wrong tense)
3) I bet it's just because poor dad has fang ache.
4) *Own answer*

Links to writing
1), 2), 3), 4) *Own answers*

18 How authors use language
Comprehension
1) Bits of string and catnip.
2) Cats only play with special cat toys – their owners. They only play to please us.
3) Cat food can come out of tins. Cats cannot open tins – they need an opener. Hence they would see their owners as performing this important function.
4) Their owners feel sorry for them and feel guilty, so they feed them more.
5) Mouse, frog, feathers. They will be messy: *'bits of …'.*
6) We are supposed to own the cat but they have such power over us that the author suggests it is the other way around.

Language focus
1), 2), 3), 4) *Own answers*

Links to writing
1), 2), 3) *Own answers*

19 Use of direct speech
Comprehension
1) A school playground in front of a brick wall.
2) Annie and Jack are sister and brother. We know this because *'Jack looked across the school playground at his sister.'*
3) Annie seems to be talking to someone who isn't there.
4) Jack saw Annie nodding her head and smiling at the empty space next to her. She was waving her hands around.
5) Her brother isn't surprised and doesn't particularly care what his sister does.
6) Annie is with her imaginary friend Sarah.
7) Annie's friend is an invisible time traveller.
8) Saying something in a sneering or cutting way.

Language focus
1) New speaker, new paragraph
Open and close speech marks
Commas before speech starts
Full stop or other final punctuation inside the speech marks
2) *Own answer*
3) Annie was nodding and smiling at her *'friend'* so she was enjoying being with her. When she introduces her *'friend'* to Jack, she has a pleased look on her face. Jack is embarrassed and fed up so he *'mutters'* in reply. Annie *'retorted, unruffled'* in reply to show that she doesn't care what Jack thinks. She *'opened her eyes wide, and gave him a superior stare'* to show that she knows best.

Links to writing
1), 2) *Own answers*

20 Test your grammar, punctuation and spelling
Grammar
Cohesion within paragraphs
Evie went home early but found she had no key. <u>Firstly</u>, she tried not to panic <u>and then</u> she panicked! <u>After that</u>, she decided to get the spare key from her neighbour, but of course the neighbour was out. This problem needed a serious plan so she looked in her bag for her phone so she could ring someone – anyone. As she put her hand in her bag to dig out her phone, she felt the jagged edge of something that felt like a <u>key</u> … yes, it was the <u>key</u>. She felt stupid but let herself into the flat and thought no more about it. <u>Later</u>, when she was locking up to go to bed, she couldn't find her <u>key</u> <u>because</u> … she had left it outside in the lock! It was not a good day.

Punctuation
Brackets to add a comment or information
1), 3), 5) and **6)**
Brackets to explain the meaning of a word
1) David Beckham is a sports celebrity (a person others are interested in day-to-day media) who has a life of fame and fortune.
2) He wants to be a landscape architect (a person who creates the landscape around us) in the future.
3) The office needs to recruit a plumber (a tradesperson who specialises in installing and maintaining systems used for drinking water, sewage and drainage).
4) An engineer needs specific skills (scientific knowledge, mathematics, problem solving) for solving technical, social and economic problems.
5) A computer systems analyst is a job in the field of information technology (solving problems related to computers).
6) Physicians (treat patients), dentists (teeth), podiatrists (foot care) and veterinarians (animals) are all specialist surgeons.

Spelling
Plurals
1) geese
2) knives
3) taxis
4) potatoes
5) pianos
6) analyses

Homophones
1) threw
2) practised
3) guest
4) peace
5) fought
6) morning; Isle

21 Common errors
Comprehension
1) Different spellings are used if the same-sounding word is used as a verb or a noun.
2) Mostly if the noun contains a c then the verb will have an s, e.g.:
some practice > to practise.
3) E.g. device/devise; advice/advise
4) They're/there/their; it's/its; who's/whose
5) *Own answers*

Language focus
1) a. It's not clear which is the best football team.
b. I went to the match, but there was no score.
c. She was not sure whose bag it was, so she handed it to the teacher.
d. It was seven minutes past three and the train had not arrived.

e. He wanted to go farther but the snow was too deep.
2) *Own answers*; licence, practice, advice, breath, bath are all nouns.
3) *Own answers*; verbs: to license, to practise, to advise, to breathe, to bathe. Note the change of spelling.
4) a. aisle in a church/isle is short for island
b. altar to be found in a church/alter is to change something
c. cereal is a grain-like corn (you may eat it for breakfast)/serial suggests that one thing follows after another (you may watch a serial on TV)
d. heard is about hearing something/herd is the collective noun for a lot of animals, e.g. cattle
e. desert is hot, dry land/dessert is a pudding

Links to writing
1) a. principle means rule or code of conduct; a principal is the head of a university or college
b. disinterested means impartial; uninterested means not interested
c. proceed means to go ahead with something; precede means to go before something (pre- is the prefix)

22 Finding new words
Comprehension
1) The author describes his hat, face, clothes, jewellery and mannerisms.
2) The author tells us the colour, size, shape of the features he describes.
3) The author uses interesting and unusual adjectives to describe these things.
4) *'He grinned a lot'*
'a habit of flopping his hand at you while he was talking'
'wriggling sort of chap'
5) *'narrow eyes'*
'bad teeth'
'perfectly ghastly tie'
6) He is dressed up like an eel, he has a foxy sort of face and his suit is like drawing-room curtains.

Language focus
1) Hostile – angry; remedy – cure; miserable – unhappy; minute – tiny; funny – witty
2) The words need discussing. They may be seen in different favourable/unfavourable lights according to the context.

Favourable	Unfavourable
quaint, extraordinary, fantastic, curious, unique	strange, unusual, uncommon, unfamiliar, peculiar, irregular, abnormal

3) *Own answers*

Links to writing
1) *Own answer*

23 Paragraphs and order
Comprehension
1) *'Before money was invented people had to buy and sell by exchanging things.'*
2) The problem with the system was that you had to find somebody who wanted what you had to exchange.
3) Blocks of salt, shells and beads have all been used as forms of money.
4) Money has been made out of gold, silver and copper.
5) The weight of a coin was important because the value of a coin depended on

that it is easier to read. Newspapers rely on visual impact on the page as well as the content.

Links to writing
1), 2) *Own answers*

12 Instructions
Comprehension
1) The title clearly tells the reader what the instructions are for.
2) Sub-headings are useful to break down the instructions into understandable sections. For example, *'You will need ½ cup of self-raising flour. You will need 1½ teaspoons of baking powder. You will need a pinch of salt …'* This clearly becomes repetitive and obscures the useful information.
3) The features in the instructions that make it easy to use include: bullet points, numbering, diagrams and illustrations.
4) It would be impossible to make biscuits.

Language focus
1), 2), *Own answers*
3) Using numbers in instructions suggests the logical order of what needs to be done, i.e. point 2 follows point 1. Connectives need to be chosen carefully to suggest the process, e.g.: first … then … next … finally.

Links to writing
1), 2), 3) *Own answers*

13 Test your grammar, punctuation and spelling
Grammar

Relative clauses using who, which, where *and* why
1) where
2) who
3) which
4) who
5) which
6) where
7) who
8) which; why

Punctuation

Hyphens
Accept all correct and reasonable sentences.

Dashes to add a comment or information
1) This camera – top of the range don't you know – is on my birthday list.
2) We're off school this Friday – we always have an inset day at this time of year – so I can catch up then.
3) I love football – I try really hard – so I always get selected for the team.
4) Netball – a game played more by girls than boys for some reason – is so much fun.
5) Ellen – the tall girl at the back with blonde hair – is very popular in our class.
6) Lacrosse is a game they play at the school on the hill – they would, wouldn't they – but we play hockey.

Spelling

Spelling confusable words
1) available
2) relevant
3) symbol
4) especially
5) vegetable
6) vehicle

Silent letters
1) knife, whistle, scissors, gnome, thumb, salmon
2) wheel, island, castle, plumber, knot, palm tree

14 Relative clauses
Comprehension
1) They are made up of a series of simple sentences.
2) Information is added about where, why and who.
3) It helps you understand the focus of each clause, e.g. **who** is used for people but **whose** suggests something belongs to somebody.
4) The teacher picked up the book **what** had the cover torn off. Should be *which* – one thing is in relationship to another.
He had a row with his mother **that** was very cross. Should be *who* – a person is the subject.
I made up my mind **what** I would like to go on my holiday. Should be *where* or *why*. *What* suggests no relationship between the two clauses.

Language focus
1) **a.** Reuben has a new girlfriend who is a champion swimmer.
b. I am going to see my sister who is older than me.
c. The tree blew in the wind, which had been blowing hard all day.
d. He returned the t-shirt to the shop that was too big for him.
e. I talked to the girl whose hair was bright red.
f. He was sent to see the head teacher, who told him off.
g. In the playground, I saw John, whose leg was in plaster.
h. He could not understand why it had not happened to him.
i. My uncle owns a car, which is always breaking down.
j. The detectives never knew why the men had robbed the bank.

Links to writing
1) **a.** The boy whose arm was caught in the door struggled to get it free.
b. The girl whose bike had been lost phoned the police.
c. The boxer who was knocked out in the ring had not been good enough.
d. The doctor who had been on call arrived too late to deliver the baby.
e. The computer game, which had only been bought last week, was broken.
2) Various answers are possible.

15 Letters
Comprehension
1) So that the person you wrote to knows who the letter has come from and how to get in contact with the writer.
2) The date is important because it allows the reader to place the letter in context of other events.
3) Dear Sir/Madam (when the writer is unsure of the recipient's gender and name)
Dear Mr Smith (formal – when the person is known to the writer)
Dear Claire (informal – when the person is known to the writer)
4) Yours faithfully (formal – when the person is unknown to the writer)
Yours sincerely (formal – when the person is known to the writer)
Yours truly (informal – when the person is known to the writer)
5) *'We all enjoy PE and games and this playing field is the only place the school has to carry out these activities.'*
'Our teacher says that it is the law to teach PE but we will have nowhere to do this.'
'My mum says she will not be able to pick

me up from this field after school because it is too far away from where she works.'
6) Dominic's tone is nice and polite.

Language focus
1) The children enjoy PE and games.
It is the law for the school to teach PE. It will cost the school a lot of money to transport the children to and from school.
His mum will not be able to pick him up from the playing fields.
2) *Own answers*
3) **a.** Queen's Drive
Belfast
ABC 123
b. Prince Walk
London
W3 4RR
c. Water Street
Manchester
1 2WW

Links to writing
1), 2) *Own answers*

16 Performing for meaning
Comprehension
1) The author plays with the 'cheet/cheat' sound in spelling. The poem makes fun of the difficulties in the sounds of English words and how this can cause confusion.
2) It is not true that a monkey is a monk just because the same sound is in both words.
3) The large bird (turkey) has nothing to do with a person from the country Turkey (a Turk) just because the same letters and sound appear in both words.
4) A springbok is a deer-like animal from South Africa. It has nothing to do with the season just because the same word/sound appears in both. In the same way, a walrus has nothing to do with a wall.
5) The writer creates humour – 'bad' is in 'badger' but the animal does not have this characteristic. 'Add' is in 'adder' but the snake could never have this human skill. Other answers are not prescriptive. Children should note that where they stress words in a sentence changes its meaning and effect.

Language focus
1), 2), 3), 4), 5) *Own answers*
Links to writing
1), 2) *Own answers*

17 Edit and improve your work
Comprehension
1) Little Wolf was writing this letter to let his parents know how things are going at school.
2) The school isn't open yet and Uncle Bigbad is being awkward.
3) Dad has a fang ache instead of a toothache. Also, Little Wolf says *'Paws crossed'* instead of *'Fingers crossed'*.
4) *'grrrish', 'soonly', 'wunce', 'orkwood'*
5) cross, soon, once, awkward
6) To emphasise them and bring them to the reader's attention or to mimic shouting in a verbal conversation.

Language focus
1) **a.** I'll teach you. (wrong verb)
b. You were the first. (the verb must agree with the subject)
c. I don't know anything. (double negative)
d. The book that I read. (**that** is demonstrative but **what** is a question)
e. He did it (the verb must agree with the subject)

Parenthesis

	Explain a word	Emphasise a point	Show what the writer is thinking	Add extra information
, who was short and very funny,				yes
– and I mean really funny –		yes	yes	
(a person who tells jokes)	yes			
– that is a true story by the way.		yes		yes
(you know the sort of joke I mean)			yes	
, he's a friend of mine,				yes
(though I don't believe that)			yes	

Spelling

Useful words

1) forty
2) committee
3) rhythm
4) appreciate
5) correspond
6) awkward

Easily confused words

Accept all correct and reasonable sentences.

Comprehension

1) Why is it important to put your address in a letter?

2) Why is the date important?

3) What ways are there to start a letter besides 'Dear Sir'? When would you use them?

4) What ways are there to end a letter besides 'Yours faithfully'? When would you use them?

5) List three arguments that Dominic uses to convince the builders.

6) Does Dominic sound nice or nasty in the tone of his writing?

Language focus

1) List the arguments that the writer uses in this letter. Can you suggest some better ones?

2) In an argument you can use words or phrases to suggest an alternative. Use each of these in a sentence to show this.
   a. but
   b. however
   c. some people argue that
   d. it could be argued that

3) Write out the following addresses as they should appear on a letter.
   a. queens drive Belfast abc 123
   b. prince walk London w3 4rr
   c. water st Manchester 1 2ww

Links to writing

1) Imagine you work for the building company and you write a reply to Dominic's letter. Use the style tips.
   What arguments would you use?
   Write a paragraph for each argument. Give examples.
   Set the letter out correctly.
   Use some of the words useful for arguments given above.

2) Write the letter using a computer, print it and sign it. You could role-play the reaction in the class when the letter is received. What would your friends say to oppose the arguments?

16 Performing for meaning

Practise reading the following poem so that you can perform it.

The cheetah, my dearest, is known not to cheat

The cheetah, my dearest, is known not to cheat;
the tiger possesses no tie;
the horse-fly, of course, was never a horse;
the lion will not tell a lie.

The turkey, though perky, was never a Turk;
nor the monkey ever a monk;
the mandrel*, though like one, was never a man,
but some men are like him, when drunk.

The springbok, dear thing, was not born in the spring;
the walrus will not build a wall.
No badger is bad; no adder can add.
There is no truth in these things at all.

George Barker

*A spindle on a machine, enabling things to turn around.

Speak about it

What point is the writer trying to make about the English language?
Is this poem funny or serious?
Why would it be important to perform this poem correctly to get the right effect?
How important will it be to stress the rhymes in the poem?
Can you work out the pattern of rhyme?

Comprehension

1) 'The **cheetah**, my dearest, is known not to **cheat**'. What sound is the author playing with in the first line? What point is he making about English?

2) Look at the line: 'nor the monkey ever a monk'. The poet says, 'There is no truth in these things at all'. What does he really mean?

3) Why was the turkey 'never a Turk'?

4) What is a springbok? Why has it nothing to do with spring? What is a walrus? Why has this nothing to do with a wall?

5) Explain how the writer plays with words to do with a badger and an adder.

Language focus

1) Where you place stress on various words can really influence your performance. Read the following but stress the word in bold. What differences are there?

   No badger is bad

   No **badger** is bad

   No badger **is** bad

   No badger is **bad**

2) Try the same exercise but use: 'no adder can add' and 'There is no truth in these things at all'.

3) Read the first verse aloud, but this time lower your voice on certain words. What happens? Try this again but increase the volume. What happens?

4) What happens if you slow down or speed up in places? Read the bold words slowly and the rest fast. Which is the best version?

   The cheetah, **my dearest**, is known not to cheat.

   The cheetah, my dearest, is known not to cheat.

   The cheetah, my dearest, is known **not to cheat.**

5) Try the same exercise but use another few lines from the poem. Perform them in front of some others and listen to what they say about it.

Links to writing

1) Use the following words to write and perform a new verse for the poem.
   hedgehog   gooseberry   steeplechase   palm tree

2) Write a guide to reading aloud and performing poems, using some of the techniques that you have learned in this unit. How do you make sure readers are using appropriate intonation and volume so that the meaning is clear?

17 Edit and improve your work

Little Wolf's Haunted Hall for Small Horrors

In this story, scary wolves are opening a scary new school.
Here is Little Wolf's letter home.

Dear Mum and Dad,

Please please PLEEEEZ don't be so grrrish. It's not fair Dad keeps saying, 'GET A MOVE ON LAZYBONES, OPEN YOUR SCHOOL QUICK.' Just because he has fang ache, I bet, boo shame. Today I will do news 1st, then cheery pics for him after.

Yeller and me and Stubbs are trying. Paws crossed we open soonly. But did you forget our 1 big problem I told you about before? I will tell you wunce more. It is the ghost of Uncle Bigbad. He is fine, in a dead way, but he keeps being orkwood nasty, saying do this and do that or no more haunting from me. Just because he knows we needed him for our School Spirit.

Ian Whybrow

Comprehension

1) Why do you think Little Wolf was writing this letter?

2) What appears to be the problem at the school?

3) Which words give you a clue that the writer is not a person?

4) Which words do you not recognise?

5) Can you guess what they mean?

6) Why do you think some words are written in capital letters?

Language focus

1) Rewrite the following in correct English and explain what you think is incorrect.

   a. I'll learn you.

   b. You was the first.

   c. I don't know nothing.

   d. The book what I read.

   e. He done it.

2) Rewrite the following phrases correctly and explain what you think is incorrect.

   a. She give me

   b. the actors was

   c. My mum don't let us

   d. I never saw nobody.

   e. Tracey done her work.

3) **Just because he has fang ache, I bet, boo shame.**
   Improve this sentence and write it correctly.

4) Which words in the passage opposite are not correctly spelled? Write them correctly. You may need to check in a dictionary.

Links to writing

1) Rewrite the passage in correct English. How does this change the impression we get of Little Wolf?

2) Continue the story of how they deal with Uncle Bigbad to get the school opened. What adventures would they have?

3) What might be on the timetable in this school for 'small horrors'? Design one.

4) Imagine that you have to tell a friend who is new to the school what it is really like, and the kind of things you get up to there. Write a letter containing this information.

18 How authors use language

Is this how you expect a book about pets would be written?

The Truth About Pets: Being Owned By a Cat

Playing with cats is a problem. Forget all that stuff about bits of string and catnip. Cats only play with special cat toys. You are their special toy. And this lasts for approximately two minutes – only when you are paying attention. This is to keep you (the 'can-opener') happy; you would be sad if their stomachs were rumbling.

And the thing to remember is that cats are the most intelligent of beasts. One day they will go back to their own planet; consider what they will tell the others about how stupid human beings are.

So … what games do cats play with you? It's never the other way around. Only you think it is.

1. **Cat square-dance**. Cats will sit in defined areas. On mats. On your clean washing. On the steps in front of you. On the most comfortable chair in the garden; this will be the one you want to sit in.

2. **Wet cement**. They will seek it out and mark this territory with their paws.

3. **Keeping an eye on the food cupboard or fridge**. Some days they will just sit there looking cuddly, staring at the food place; big round eyes will make you feel guilty. You know that you have been starving them so you will immediately fill their food bowl.

4. **Bringing you gifts**. These are, in fact, just the remains of their lunch – bits of old mouse or frog; maybe a feather or two if you are lucky. They will be messy – but you will be thrilled by the attention.

Such is the way cats own us.

Speak about it

Who is the audience for this kind of book?
Why do you think the writer chose to write differently?
Do you find anything in the tone of the writing amusing or unusual? Why?
Find examples of short sentences. Why does the writer use them?
Find examples of longer sentences. Why does the writer choose to make them longer?
Find examples of when the writer does not use complete sentences. Why does the writer do this?

Comprehension

1) Name two things people normally use to play with cats.

2) Why does the author say that these do not work?

3) Explain why cats would call their owners 'can-openers'?

4) What is the effect of the cats staring at the food cupboard or fridge?

5) What kinds of 'gifts' might cats bring their owners? What state would they be in?

6) Explain the joke in the title: 'Being Owned By a Cat'.

Language focus

1) In this passage the author constructs shorter, more factual sentences to give information and to create a jokey effect for your age group. Rewrite the information as you would in a traditional non-fiction book. Which is the more interesting version for your age group? Why?

2) Use connectives to join the sentences in the first paragraph into one or two longer ones. Does the effect of the writing change?

3) Why does the writer start some of the sentences with 'And'?

4) Look at the short sentences in the numbered points. Rewrite these as one or two long sentences. What happens to the effect of the writer even if the facts do not change?

Links to writing

1) Write your own 'The Truth About Pets' page for some animal behaviours that need explaining to younger children.
Choose an animal that they will know. Think about the kind of things they do.
Decide what will go in each paragraph.
Find out the real animal facts.
Use informal rather than formal language.
Keep the sentences short.
Use semicolons to create sentences that are jokes.

2) Publish your page, using the computer and any visuals that you can find.

3) See how successful you have been. Test the story on younger children: did they like it? Did they find it easy to understand?

19 Use of direct speech

Annie's Game

Annie was talking to someone who wasn't there.

Jack looked across the school playground at his sister. She was nodding her head and smiling at the empty space next to her, waving her hands around as she talked. Jack wondered briefly why he wasn't surprised. Nothing Annie did ought to surprise him any more. She was capable of anything, including having a conversation with thin air. Not that he cared what Annie was up to.

'Annie!' he called. 'Go and sit on the wall.'

Annie gave him a big smile.

'Can Sarah come with me?'

'What?' Jack turned to his sister.

'I said, "Can Sarah come with me?"'

'Sarah who?'

'Sarah Slade.' Annie pointed at the empty space next to her, a pleased look on her face.

'This is Sarah. She's my new friend. Say hello to Sarah, Jack.'

'There's no-one there,' Jack muttered.

'Yes there is,' Annie retorted, unruffled. 'She's just invisible, that's all.'

'Of course she is,' said Jack. 'Silly me. I should have realised.'

'Don't be sarcastic, Jack.' Annie opened her eyes wide, and gave him a superior stare. 'Sarah's a time-traveller you know. She's come to visit me from the future.'

Jack resisted a desire to bang his head against the nearest brick wall. It was a feeling he often had when he was alone with Annie.

Narinder Dhami

Speak about it

Who is speaking here? How do you know?
Do you always need to tell your reader who is speaking?
Why is special punctuation necessary to show speech?
Are there any special features of how speech is set out?
How is this different from when you look at a playscript?

Comprehension

1) Where does the scene take place?

2) What is the relationship between Annie and Jack? Find the words that tell you.

3) What do you think is strange about Annie's behaviour?

4) What can Jack see her doing?

5) How does her brother react at first?

6) Who is Annie with?

7) What information do we learn about her **friend**?

8) What does **sarcastic** mean? You may need to look in a dictionary.

Language focus

1) List any features you notice about how to punctuate speech, e.g. setting it out, position of punctuation.

2) Some words (adverbs) tell us the tone of voice of the speaker, e.g. **the man said indignantly**, **he replied impatiently**. Rewrite five speech sentences from the passage and include adverbs to show how Annie or Jack felt.

3) List any actions in the passage that show us how the characters feel about the situation.

Links to writing

1) The words people use tell us about how they feel. The way that the author reports those words also tells us about characters. Continue with the story opposite using some speech. Give us information as well, as the author would. How does Jack react? What is the reason for Annie's behaviour?

2) Speech creates a sense of character. Imagine someone in your class behaves like Annie, but her story turns out to be true. Write the story, which should include some speech. Show why you don't believe her at first. What has to happen before you know it's true? How do you feel then? If you use a computer, it will be easier to put new speakers on new lines.

20 Test your grammar, punctuation and spelling

Grammar

Cohesion within paragraphs

Find and write the words that help to build cohesion in this paragraph.

Evie went home early but found she had no key. Firstly, she tried not to panic and then she panicked! After that, she decided to get the spare key from her neighbour, but of course the neighbour was out. This problem needed a serious plan so she looked in her bag for her phone so she could ring someone – anyone. As she put her hand in her bag to dig out her phone, she felt the jagged edge of something that felt like a key … yes, it was the key. She felt stupid but let herself into the flat and thought no more about it. Later, when she was locking up to go to bed, she couldn't find her key because … she had left it outside in the lock! It was not a good day.

Punctuation

Brackets to add a comment or information

Write the sentences in which brackets are used correctly to add extra information.

1) Adele (being excellent at music) had always won the music award.

2) The bike which was new (had been a birthday present).

3) Some people (usually the boring ones) do this the same way every week.

4) John and Dan always (got the bus) to town.

5) The Olympic Stadium (which is in London) is an awesome structure.

6) *The Angel of the North* (a sculpture in Gateshead) was designed by Antony Gormley.

Brackets to explain the meaning of a word

Add brackets to the sentences to explain the meanings of words.

1) David Beckham is a sports celebrity a person others are interested in, in day-to-day media who has a life of fame and fortune.

2) He wants to be a landscape architect a person who creates the landscape around us in the future.

3) The office needs to recruit a plumber a tradesperson who specialises in installing and maintaining systems used for drinking water, sewage and drainage.

4) An engineer needs specific skills scientific knowledge, mathematics, problem solving for solving technical, social and economic problems.

5) A computer systems analyst is a job in the field of information technology solving problems related to computers.

6) Physicians treat patients, dentists teeth, podiatrists foot care and veterinarians animals are all specialist surgeons.

Spelling

Plurals

Write the plural.

Example   person → people

1) goose

2) knife

3) taxi

4) potato

5) piano

6) analysis

Homophones

Choose the right homophone to complete the sentence and write it.

1) He (**threw/through**) the ball to his friend.

2) She (**practised/practiced**) the piano daily.

3) It's important to be on the (**guest/guessed**) list.

4) Give (**piece/peace**) a chance.

5) They (**fort/fought**) like cat and dog.

6) It was a beautiful clear (**mourning/morning**) on the (**Aisle/Isle**) of Skye.

21 Common errors

Many words sound the same but mean something different and can be spelled differently. These are called homophones**.**

How can you be sure that you are using the correct word?
Sometimes knowing some grammar can help.

Example 1

Noun	Verb
some advice	to advise
some practice	to practise
a licence	to license
an effect	to affect
the past	it passed

Example 2

- **Who's** is a short form (contraction) of **who is**.

    Who's that strange person over there?

- **Whose** is a pronoun suggesting **that which belongs to**.

    Whose car is this?

    That is the boy **whose** mother won the lottery.

Example 3

- **Their** tells you **something belongs to someone**:

    Their house is bigger than ours.

- **They're** is a shortened version of **they are**.

    They're not coming to the party because you upset them.

- **There** tells us **in** or **at that place**.

    Stand over **there**.

    It can also draw attention to someone or something.

    There goes John.

    Or it can introduce a sentence or clause.

    There seem to be only eggs left on the shelf.

Other examples you will just have to learn!

    Station**ary** (to be still)   Station**ery** (paper, pens, etc.)

Try remembering: **e** is in l**e**tter. You need station**ery** to write **letters**.

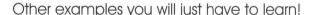

Speak about it

You can tell what **homophone** means because it is made up of two parts: **homo-** meaning 'same' and **-phone**. What does this suffix mean?
What other words can you think of that have **-phone** in them? Do they help to prove that the meaning you have discovered is correct?
What other handy tips do you use to help remember confusing words?

Comprehension

1) Why might grammar be helpful in showing you how to spell homophones?

2) What spelling rule do you notice when certain words are used as a noun and then a verb? How does the spelling change?

3) Can you think of any more words that might follow the same rule?

4) What other words can you think of where the shortened form (using an apostrophe) may cause some problems with words sounding the same but meaning something different?

5) Something that helps you remember how to spell something tricky, such as 'e *is in letter. You need stationery to write letters*', is called a **mnemonic**. Can you think of any other mnemonics that you use?

Language focus

1) Write the following sentences using the correct word from the choices. Use a dictionary to help.

   a. (**Its/it's**) not clear which is the best football team.

   b. I went to the match, but (**there/their/they're**) was no score.

   c. She was not sure (**whose/who's**) bag it was, so she handed it to the teacher.

   d. It was seven minutes (**passed/past**) three and the train had not arrived.

   e. He wanted to go (**father/farther**) but the snow was too deep.

2) Use the following words in sentences to show their meaning. Identify whether they are being used as a noun, verb or adjective.

   licence   practice   advice   breath   bath

3) Now write sentences using each word as a verb. Use a dictionary to help. What differences do you notice in spelling?

4) Explain the difference in meaning between each of the two words below. Write sentences to show that you understand the different meanings.

   a. aisle/isle **b.** altar/alter **c.** cereal/serial **d.** heard/herd **e.** desert/dessert

Links to writing

1) Some words can be confusing. Write a story that shows the confusion caused when one of the words was used wrongly. Find the meanings first to show you know the difference between them.

   a. principle/principal   **b.** disinterested/uninterested   **c.** proceed/precede

22 Finding new words

THE OTTERBURY INCIDENT

Johnny Sharp wore a grey homburg hat, rather on the back of his head and cocked sideways, with the brim turned down in front. He had a foxy sort of face - narrow eyes, long thin nose, long thin lips; he grinned a lot, allowing his bad teeth and gold-stopped one on the left of his upper jaw to show. He had a loud checked suit with padded shoulders, and a perfectly ghastly tie with large patterns on it like drawing-room curtains. He had two flashy rings on his right hand, and a habit of flopping his hand at you while he was talking. He was a narrow, wriggling sort of a chap, from top to bottom; like a dressed-up eel. Or a snake.

C Day Lewis

Speak about it

When you are describing someone, why is detail necessary?

What are adjectives?

How can you find alternatives to them so you do not use the same word every time?

What is a thesaurus? How is it different from a dictionary?

How do you find the words that you want?

Do the adjectives chosen in the passage make you like or dislike this person?

Comprehension

1) List the features that the author chooses to describe, e.g. hat, face, etc.

2) What details does the author choose to give about those features?

3) What kind of adjectives does he use to describe shape, size, colour, etc.?

4) He also describes the character's mannerisms. Find some examples.

5) Which words tell you that the author does not like Johnny?

6) Which comparisons tell you this as well?

Language focus

1) A thesaurus helps you to find **synonyms** – words of a similar meaning. Select the word on the right that has the most similar meaning to the word on the left.

hostile	red, sunny, angry, sensible
remedy	cure, ugly, stout, permanent
miserable	playful, unhappy, tall, stormy
minute	tiny, huge, sad, foolish
funny	stupid, successful, witty, nice

2) These words are found in a thesaurus under 'odd'. Find out the meanings of the words. How do they give a different impression of 'odd'? Put them in two columns: **Favourable** and **Unfavourable**.

> quaint   strange   unusual   uncommon   unfamiliar
> extraordinary   fantastic   peculiar   curious
> irregular   abnormal   unique

Links to writing

1) Write a description for the police of a pet that is lost. This should concentrate on the facts only. Write the same description as if you did not like the animal. Which adjectives will you choose to show your feelings? Use a thesaurus to find new words.

23 Paragraphs and order

Money

Before money was invented, people had to buy and sell by exchanging things. A farmer might exchange his surplus wheat for a horse or a cow that one of his neighbours did not need; but first he had to find another farmer who wanted wheat and who had a horse or cow to spare.

Even after money was invented, it was not always the convenient shape that it is today. In the past, many things have been used for money – blocks of salt, shells and beads.

Eventually, people realised that metal was the most suitable substance to make money from. It was valuable, did not wear out and could be made into convenient sizes. Gold, silver and copper were the three metals most commonly used. The value of the coin was the value of the amount of gold, silver or copper that it contained, so every time business took place the coins had to be weighed.

The next stage was to make coins in a much wider range of weights. These weights, and a symbol of the country, were stamped on the coins.

Today, coins are valuable, but not because they are made of valuable metals; there are no gold coins made today. Coins and paper money have value because a government has agreed that each note or coin shall be worth its face value, which is the amount stamped on it.

Why is it important to write in paragraphs?
If this passage was not written in paragraphs, would it be as easy to read?
How do we know when to end one paragraph and start another?
What is each of these five paragraphs about?
If you were to change the order of the paragraphs here, would it make a difference?

Comprehension

1) What did people do before money was invented?

2) What was the problem with this system?

3) What strange things have been used as a form of money?

4) What kinds of metal has money been made out of?

5) Why was the weight of a coin important?

6) How do we know the value of present-day coins?

Language focus

1) Identify the sentence (topic sentence) that tells you what each paragraph will be about. Write it at the centre of a spider diagram and write notes around it, using the detail in each paragraph.

2) Look at the words that begin each paragraph. Identify clues that tell you the paragraphs are in the right time order.

3) Read the paragraphs in a different order. Does the passage make sense now? Why not?

4) Write four paragraphs about the history of something else, e.g. toys, computers, football. (You may need to do some research on your topic.) Use the following words to start your paragraphs.

before   eventually   the next stage   today

Links to writing

1) Describe in three paragraphs the place where you live. Use the following plan.

   a. In the first paragraph, describe the whole area and its features.

   b. In the second paragraph, describe one part of this area.

   c. In the third paragraph, describe one small thing in this part.

   In this way, you are acting like a camera, zooming in on something.

   Check that you are using paragraphs correctly, that you have a topic sentence and that when you talk about something new, you start a new paragraph.

24 Changing the order of sentences

Surnames

Did you ever wonder where the word 'surname' comes from? The prefix **sur-** means 'over and above' or 'additional to', and surnames are additional names, or names added to a child's personal name. A child's surname was not always the same as his or her father's; in the Middle Ages, surnames were a kind of nickname and might have come from the work that a person did or from where they lived.

Perhaps the commonest surnames are occupational names. In the past, a Smith was a man who smited or worked in metal, so today we have names such as Goldsmith – a man who smited in gold. A Wright was a man who worked with wood; a Mason worked in stone, and the origin of names such as Taylor and Thatcher are obvious.

Surnames that were the names of natural features in the country also became common. Before there were addresses in the countryside there might have been two Richards in the same area – one living near a wood and one near a field. So they became Richard Woods and Richard Field to distinguish them.

Speak about it

Which sentence tells you what each of these paragraphs is really about?
What does the rest of the paragraph add to this?
Experiment with reading the sentences in a different order. Talk about whether the paragraph still makes sense and why.

Comprehension

1) Why were people given surnames? In which paragraph did you find the information?

2) Where does **surname** come from? In which paragraph did you find the information?

3) Mention two ways in which surnames were formed. In which paragraph did you find the information?

4) Using the information in the passage, decide which one is the odd one out in each group and say why.

    a. Mason Johnson Painter Tyler   **c.** Moore Dale Hill Smith

    b. Goldsmith Baxter Brook

Language focus

1) The following paragraph needs to be broken up into sentences.

Every other Monday I go to my Club but we are moving soon to a new house and I think I will have to stop going because of the journey which would be pleasant in summer but not good in winter when the nights are cold and dark especially if you like sitting in front of the TV like me.

2) On the opposite page, paragraph 1 contains three sentences. Number them 1, 2 and 3. Rewrite them in a different order. What happens to the sense of the paragraph if you write them in the order of 2, 1, 3 or 2, 3, 1? Why does the writer start the paragraph with the question? What do the other sentences do?

3) Try this with the other two paragraphs. What happens to the sense? What conclusions can you draw about the order of sentences?

Links to writing

1) Write the topic sentences in the three paragraphs on the opposite page. List under them, in note form, the more-detailed information given. You could do this as a spider diagram.

2) Suppose a fourth topic sentence was: In modern times, other cultures have settled in Britain and brought in new names. Give some detail to illustrate this.

3) Use the following two sets of sentences as topic sentences. Write more about each paragraph but write notes to start with. (You could do this on a computer so that it will be easier to rewrite your notes as sentences. You may need to do some research.)

    a. It is hot in Africa during the day. The nights are often cold.

    b. Venice is a famous city. It is in Italy. It has canals and no roads.

25 Speech marks (inverted commas)

The Adventures of Tom Sawyer

About noon the next day the boys arrived at the dead tree; they had come for their tools. Tom was impatient to go to the haunted house. Huck Finn suddenly said …

'Looky here Tom, do you know what day it is?'

Tom ran mentally over the days of the week and then quickly lifted his eyes with a startled look in them.

'My! I never once thought of it, Huck.'

'Well, I didn't neither, but all at once it popped on me that it was Friday.'

'Blame it; a body can't be too careful, Huck. We might 'a' got into an awful scrape, tackling such things on a Friday.'

'*Might*! Better say we *would*! There's some lucky days, maybe, but Friday ain't.'

'Any fool knows that. I don't reckon YOU was the first that found it out, Huck.'

'Well, I never said I was, did I? And Friday ain't all, neither. I had a rotten dream last night … dreamt about rats.'

'No! Sure sign of trouble. Did they fight?'

'No.'

'Well, that's good, Huck. When they don't fight, it's only a sign that there's trouble around, you know. All we got to do is look mighty sharp and keep out of it. We'll drop this thing for today, and play. Do you know Robin Hood, Huck?'

'No. Who's Robin Hood?'

'Why he was one of the greatest men that ever lived in England … and the best. … We'll play Robin Hood … it's nobby fun. I'll learn you.'

'I'm agreed.'

So they played Robin Hood all the afternoon, now and then casting a yearning eye down upon the haunted house.

Mark Twain

Speak about it

Why is special punctuation necessary to show speech?

Are there any special features of how speech is set out?

How is this different from when you look at a playscript?

Who is speaking here? How do you know?

Do you always need to tell your reader who is speaking?

Comprehension

1) Name the two characters speaking in the passage.

2) Why have they met by the dead tree?

3) What stops them going to the house?

4) What is their view of Friday?

5) Do you find this strange? Why?

6) What else happened to make them concerned?

7) How do you know who is speaking each time?

Language focus

1) List any features you notice about how to punctuate speech, e.g. setting it out, position of punctuation.

2) Punctuate this passage correctly.

Look out warned the passenger

Whats the matter muttered the driver half asleep

Sorry the passenger answered apologetically I thought you were going to crash

3) We can use verbs other than **said** to tell us how the speaker felt, e.g. he growled, the man shouted, he pleaded. Use the following in some speech sentences rather than **said**.

a. yelled   **c.** sobbed   **e.** roared

b. murmured   **d.** whispered

Links to writing

1) In speech you can use non-standard English. Find examples of this in the passage. Write them out correctly. What difference does it make to your view of the character?

2) Imagine that Huck and Tom come back the next day to visit the house. Write about what happens. Use speech, employing the features of speech that you noticed.

3) Using the computer, write a set of rules for the punctuation of speech that can be displayed in your classroom. Find images that you can use that will make the rules attractive and mean that others understand them better.

26 Apostrophes

King Arthur

King Arthur was dying. He'd lost the great battle and many of his knights were dead. Only Launcelot's friends, brave Sir Lucan and Sir Bedivere were left.

Camelot's castles were visible in the mist, as the two knights carried the King's body to his last resting place. They found a little deserted chapel. The King's voice was faint and he sighed as he looked up at the last Knights of the Round Table.

'We're all that's left,' he said. 'Don't feel sad. There is one final duty that you, Sir Bedivere, must perform for me.'

'Anything, my King,' said the knight. 'I'm here to serve you.'

'My time's short. Take my sword, Excalibur, which I pulled from the stone when I was a boy. It must be returned to the Lady of the Lake. Walk yonder a mile from here and you'll find a large lake. Throw the sword into the water. Return and tell me what you see.' The King turned in pain as he produced the magnificent Excalibur. It was the most powerful sword in the world, and had magical powers. Its hilt was covered in precious stones.

Sir Bedivere said, 'My Lord. You're my King,' and lifting the sword delicately in his hands, he walked away over the mountains.

He found the lake as the King had said, but just as he was about to throw the sword into the dark waters, he heard a voice in his ear.

'Don't throw this power away. It could be all yours. How will the King know? He's almost dead.'

Sir Bedivere thought for a while and the voice's power took over his mind. He betrayed his King and broke his knight's vows. He hid the sword in a bush and returned to the King.

'What did you see my brave knight?' asked Arthur, struggling to raise himself from the ground.

'Nothing, my liege, but the water's ripple as I threw in the sword.'

'Liar and traitor! You have betrayed all the knights' trust!' screamed the King.

He knew that the Lady of the Lake's bargain was to reclaim her gift to him.

Speak about it

Why do writers use apostrophes?
Are they really useful in sentences?
Do apostrophes always come before an *s*?
What would happen if you removed the apostrophes – would it make a difference to your understanding of the passage?
What problems would this cause?

Comprehension

1) Name the only two knights left.

2) Where did they take King Arthur? Why?

3) What does he ask Sir Bedivere to do?

4) What happens when Sir Bedivere tries to do it?

5) What does Sir Bedivere tell King Arthur?

6) How does the King react?

Language focus

1) Identify where apostrophes are used in the passage. Sort the examples into two columns: **Showing possession** and **Apostrophe for contraction** (letters left out).

2) Write out the shortened forms of the following words with their apostrophes.
a. cannot	**c.** what has	**e.** they have
b. it is	**d.** I have	**f.** they are

3) Match up the words in the two columns. You will first have to use the words **of the** and then put in an apostrophe, e.g. the frame of the picture – the picture's frame.

a. the frame   dresses

b. a dog   anchors

c. two ships   book

d. the ladies   picture

e. the author   paintings

f. many artists   collar

Links to writing

1) Put the apostrophes in two different places in these examples and explain the difference in meaning.
a. the cats kittens	**c.** the girls dresses
b. my brothers books	**d.** the farmers fields

2) You have to teach other pupils in the class about apostrophes. Create a character called **Super Apostrophe** to make things fun. Write his adventures with words. Remember – you have to tell people where, how and why to use apostrophes.

27 Dashes or brackets

From *Pickwick Papers*

In this story, set in Victorian times, Mr Jingle speaks in a very strange way. He is just about to travel on an open-topped coach, drawn by horses.

'Any luggage, Sir?' enquired the coachman.

'Who – I? Brown paper parcel here, that's all – other luggage gone by water – packing cases, nailed up – big as houses – heavy, very heavy,' replied the stranger, as he forced into his pocket as much as he could of the brown paper parcel, which presented suspicions of containing one shirt and a handkerchief.

'Heads, heads, take care of your heads,' cried the stranger, as they came out under the low archway, which in those days formed the entrance to the coach-yard. 'Terrible place – dangerous work – other day – five children – mother – tall lady, eating sandwiches – forgot the arch – crash – knock – children look round – mother's head off – sandwich in her hand – no mouth to put it in – head of a family off – shocking, shocking – eh, sir, eh?'

Charles Dickens

Speak about it

What do you notice immediately about the look of the final paragraph when dashes are used?
What kind of effect does it give when you read it?
Is it amusing? Why?
Why not use full stops or commas? What would be the effect of this?
What impression does this use of this punctuation give us of the character of Mr Jingle?
Can you tell things about people's characters by the way that they speak?

Comprehension

1) What did Mr Jingle's luggage consist of?

2) What does Mr Jingle say about the rest of his luggage?

3) Do you believe Mr Jingle? Why?

4) What makes Mr Jingle tell people to 'take care of your heads'?

5) What story does Mr Jingle tell about what happened the 'other day'?

6) Is the story tragic or comic?

7) What might it say about Mr Jingle that he tells such stories?

Language focus

1) Dashes separate ideas. Rewrite the second paragraph using complete sentences to describe the same event. How does this change the effect?

2) Brackets and dashes enable writers to add more information. Add more information in the brackets to these sentences.

   a. The old man (…) left his money to the cats' home.

   b. We faced another day of snow (…).

   c. Fry the onions, add the carrots (…) and cook for two minutes.

3) Read the following sentences. Rewrite them as one sentence using brackets and dashes.

> I wanted to become a gospel singer. I had always sung gospel music with my father. He used to sing back home in Jamaica. I joined a choir in south London.

Links to writing

1) Rewrite Mr Jingle's first speech, but this time give extra information in brackets about the detail. Why had his other luggage gone by water? Why were the cases very heavy? What difference does this make to the effect of the writing?

2) Make notes about events from your past. Add information to make the recount more interesting. Use brackets for this.

3) Develop the notes you made for question 2 into a part of your autobiography and publish it using a computer.

28 Test your grammar, punctuation and spelling

Modal verbs

Complete the sentences with the verbs *might*, *should*, *will* or *must*. Use each verb at least once.

1) I _____ go to the cinema later but I don't think I'll have time.

2) I _____ go to the shops later because I'm meeting friends there.

3) I _____ go to see a friend later as I haven't seen her for a long time and she has not been well.

4) I _____ go to school tomorrow because it's the law.

5) We _____ do our homework before we leave because we have to.

Adverbs

Complete the sentences with the adverbs *perhaps*, *arguably*, *obviously*, *probably* and *surely*. Use each once.

1) I'm going to the cinema so _____ we can meet up.

2) I'm _____ the best in my class at maths.

3) I'm _____ going to China next year if I can get the money together.

4) _____ he will help you set up the stall at the fair?

5) You're _____ not a very good friend then!

Punctuation of speech (revision)

Copy each sentence and put speech marks (inverted commas) in the correct places.

1) Just mind where you are stacking those boxes, said the woman.

2) Where would you like them stacked? I asked.

3) Well, we usually have them taken upstairs, she replied.

4) Not asking for much then, I whispered under my breath.

5) Sorry, did you say something? hissed the woman.

Parenthesis

Copy and complete the chart to show what the comments in parenthesis are adding for the reader.

	Explain a word	Emphasise a point	Show what the writer is thinking	Add extra information
, who was short and very funny,				
– and I mean really funny –				
(a person who tells jokes)				
– that is a true story by the way.				
(you know the sort of joke I mean)				
, he's a friend of mine,				
(though I don't believe that)				

Spelling

Useful words

Choose and write out the correct spelling for each one.

Example

occur   okur   ocurr

1) fourty   fortee   forty

2) comitee   committee   commitee

3) rhythm   rythm   rhthm

4) apreciate   appreciatte   appreciate

5) corespond   correspond   corispond

6) awkward   akward   orkward

Easily confused words

Write a sentence for each word to show you understand the difference between them.

1) they're   **4)** who

2) their   **5)** who's

3) there   **6)** whose

Glossary

adverbial   a word or a phrase that makes the meaning of a verb more specific

ambiguity   when information is unclear because it can be interpreted in more than one way

analogy   using similarity between two words, e.g. to help you make a decision

bracket   a punctuation mark that is used in pairs to separate or add information (like this)

cohesion   joining information together

cohesive device   a term used to show how the different parts of a text fit together

dash   a punctuation mark that is used – often informally – to add a comment or information in writing. See Punctuation chart

determiner   a determiner modifies a noun, e.g. **the**, **a**, **an**, **this**, **those**, **my**, **your**, **some**, **every** or numerals

etymology   a word's history and origin

modal verb   a modal verb changes the meaning of other verbs as it tells us about how certain, able or obliged something or someone is, e.g. **will**, **would**, **can**, **could**, **may**, **might**, **shall**, **should**, **must** and **ought**

morphology   considering how a word is made up of different parts

parenthesis   an extra word, clause or sentence inserted into a passage to give non-essential information

possessive pronoun   a word that tell us who owns a noun in a sentence or phrase, e.g. **my**, **your**, **his**, **her**, **its**, **our**, **their**, **mine**, **yours**, **hers**, **ours**, **theirs**. They are determiners because they modify the noun

pronoun   a word that is often used instead of a noun or noun phrase, e.g. **I**, **you**, **he**, **she**, **it**, **we**, **they**, **this**, **who**

relative clause   a special type of subordinate clause that makes the meaning of a noun more specific by using a pronoun to link back to the noun

relative pronoun   we use relative pronouns **after** a noun, to make it clear which person or thing we are talking about or, in relative clauses, to tell us more about a person or thing, e.g. **who**, **which**, **that**, **who(m)**, **whose**

Punctuation chart

Punctuation mark word	Symbol	Note	Example
apostrophe	'	Can show that something belongs to someone or something	the girl's hat the girls' hats
		Can show that letters are missed out	can't cannot she'd she would/she had
brackets	(....)	Can be used to show that a word or phrase has been added	We said thank you (but we didn't mean it really!).
bullet point	•	Can be used to make a list clear	Things to buy: • sausages • bananas • baked beans
colon	:	Can be used before you make a list	See above.
		Can be used to give more examples after the first part of a sentence	The dogs are very funny: they are trained to do tricks.
comma	,	Can make a sentence clear or change the meaning of the sentence	Slow children crossing Slow, children crossing
		To separate the items in a list	I like sausages, bananas and baked beans.
dash	–	Can be used to add a bit more information to a sentence It's informal	The dogs are very funny – the old brown one makes me laugh.
full stop	.	Can be used at the end of a sentence to show it has finished	I went to the dog show.
		It also shows that a word is shortened or contracted	On the 23rd of Sept. I went to the dog show.

Handy hints

Spelling

Top tips on spelling

1) Try using your phonics knowledge first.

2) Does it look right? If not, what changes would make sense?

3) Use analogy: do you know another word that sounds similar and that you could use as a starting point, e.g. if it's **baby/babies**, then it's probably going to be **city/cities**.

4) If it's a long word, say the syllables; write each syllable as a chunk.

5) Use morphology: think about the root word and then about whether the word might have a prefix or a suffix that might help you to spell it, e.g. **medical** and **medicine**.

6) Use etymology: think about a word's history and, in particular, its origins in earlier forms of English or other languages to see if that might help you to spell it, e.g. **circumference** from the Latin *circumferentia* meaning the line around a circle.

7) Don't always rely on the spellcheck when working on the computer – keep thinking for yourself so that when you are writing away from technology or on your own, you don't get stuck.

Word lists

Words are taken from word lists that appear in the programmes of study and targets for the new National Curriculum [English].

accompany	definite	interrupt	rhyme
achieve	determined	leisure	sacrifice
amateur	dictionary	marvellous	shoulder
apparent	embarrass	muscle	soldier
attached	equip (-ped, -ment)	neighbour	sufficient
average	exaggerate	occupy	symbol
bargain	existence	opportunity	temperature
category	familiar	persuade	twelfth
committee	forty	prejudice	vegetable
community	government	profession	yacht
conscience	harass	pronunciation	
convenience	identity	recognise	
criticise (critic + ise)	individual	relevant	

Presentation

Top tips on handwriting

1 Keep the letters simple – no exaggerated flicks and curls.

2 Keep the letters on the line – no wandering up or down!

3 Keep the letters the same size – no huge letters appearing suddenly in the middle of a word.

4 Keep it well spaced – no huge gaps in the hope that you will have to write less, and no squashed sentences, which are hard to read.

5 Keep your capital letters and lower case letters looking different; even when they look the same, e.g. for s, the capital must be bigger than the lower case.

6 Keep the small letters the same height and the tall letters the same height (apart from *t*, which is a bit shorter than the others).

7 Letters that are tall or have tails don't need to be **very** tall or have **very** long tails; keep them under control.

8 Letters that are tall or have tails need to be straight or slanting **in the same direction**.

9 If you make a mistake then deal with it just **once**: rub it out, or put one line through it, or put it in brackets. Write the correct word clearly above it or at the side and then move on.

10 If **you** can't read it then the chances are that no one else can either. Keep it neat all the time.

Rules for capital letters

Use capital letters for:

people's names

people's titles (like **Mrs** Jones)

places

days of the week

months of the year

organisations

Full stops

Always put a full stop at the end of a sentence, unless you are using a **?** or a **!**

Rising Stars UK Ltd, 7 Hatchers Mews, Bermondsey Street, London SE1 3GS

www.risingstars-uk.com

Acknowledgements

Page 16 – Extract from *The Peppermint Pig* by Nina Bawden, published by Puffin Books 1977. Reproduced with permission of Curtis Brown, London on behalf of the Estate of Nina Bawden. Copyright © Nina Bawden, 1975.

Page 18 – Extract from *Ghosts* by Antonia Barber (copyright © Antonia Barber, 1990) reprinted by permission of A.M. Heath & Co Ltd.

Page 20 – Extract from *High Wind in Jamaica* by Richard Hughes, published by Chatto & Windus. Reprinted by permission of David Higham Associates.

Page 22 – Dennis the Menace cartoon, DC Thomson & Co. From *The Kingfisher BEANO File,* Ryhmes and Riddles by Fran Pickering, Kingfisher, 1996

Page 34 – 'The cheetah, my dearest, is known not to cheat' from *Runes and Rhymes and Tunes and Chimes* by George Barker © Estate of George Barker, published by Faber and Faber Ltd. Reprinted with permission of Faber and Faber Ltd.

Page 36– Extract from *Little Wolf's Haunted Hall for Small Horrors* by Ian Whybrow (Copyright © Ian Whybrow), Collins Children's Books. Reprinted by permission of United Agents (www.unitedagents.co.uk) on behalf of Ian Whybrow.

Page 40 – Extract from *Annie's Game* by Narinder Dhami, published by Corgi Yearling. Reprinted by permission of The Random House Group Ltd.

Page 46 – Extract from *The Otterbury Incident* by C Day Lewis, published by The Bodley Head. Reprinted by permission of Peters Fraser & Dunlop (www.petersfraserdunlop.com) on behalf of the Estate of Cecil Day Lewis.

Every effort has been made to trace copyright holders and obtain their permission for the use of copyright materials. The authors and publisher will gladly receive information enabling them to rectify any error or omission in subsequent editions.

All facts are correct at the time of going to press.

Published 2013
Text, design and layout © Rising Stars UK Ltd.

Authors: Les Ray and Gill Budgell
Educational consultant: Shareen Mayers, Routes to Success, Sutton
Text design: Green Desert Ltd
Cover design: West 8 Design
Illustrations: HL Studios
Publisher: Camilla Erskine
Copy Editor: Sarah Davies

British Library Cataloguing in Publication Data.
A CIP record for this book is available from the British Library.

ISBN: 978-0-85769-680-9

Printed by Craft Print International Ltd, Singapore